FEELING BETTER
Building Self-Esteem

Dean C. Dauw
DePaul University

Waveland Press, Inc.
Prospect Heights, Illinois

For information about this book, write or call:

Waveland Press, Inc.
P.O. Box 400
Prospect Heights, Illinois 60070
(312) 634-0081

ISBN 0-88133-157-0

Printed in the United States of America.

Contents

Preface

Giving proper recognition to all those who made this book possible is an almost impossible task.

L.S. "Barks" Barksdale set up his Barksdale Foundation for Furtherance of Human Understanding (P.O. Box 187, Idyllwild, California, 92349). He has tirelessly promoted the cause of aiding people in building their SE.

His excellent materials inspired me in the beginning when I was confronted with the challenge of learning more about SE.

He encouraged my many research efforts over the years.

Special thanks are due to all the clients and professional consultants where we conducted research at Human Resource Developers, Inc., Growth Unlimited, Inc., and SECS: Sexual Enrichment Counseling Services, Inc. (112 W. Oak, Chicago, Illinois 60610)

The professors at DePaul University were extremely supportive colleagues and the students were very cooperative.

My undying gratitude also goes to all those who are almost too numerous to mention: my loved ones, family, relatives, friends, and colleagues, and clients.

Introduction

Your self-esteem is your opinion of yourself. It is basically the sum total of all your feelings about yourself.

It plays a most important part in your life. You could compare it to a hospital life-support system of the critically ill or to a shock-absorber on a car, because your self-esteem enables you to bear up under the heartbreak of a cruel world without collapse. If you lack sufficiently strong self-esteem, you operate with a handicap. It's bad enough if everyone believes you're useless, but if you think so, too, life can become unbearable.

William James, one of the fathers of modern psychology, explored self-esteem in his *Principles of Psychology*. He defined it with this formula:

$$S.E. = \frac{Pretensions}{Successes}$$

What it comes down to is rather simple: Your S.E. depends upon how your image of your real self compares with your idealized vision of what you'd like to be. If you feel like you have come closer to achieving your ideal plans or goals for yourself, you are probably high in S.E. If you feel you have failed miserably to accomplish the goals you have set for yourself, you are likely to be low in SE.

SE does not directly affect your ability to achieve goals so much as it does your ability to enjoy what you have accomplished. The person, for example, who always wanted to be president but never got any higher than secretary of defense may feel low in SE because the achievement did not equal the ideal goal. On the other hand, the individual who always wanted to be a fashion representative may enjoy a high level of SE, if she does indeed devote her whole life to doing whatever she wants to do.

People with low SE actually may perform better than do those with high SE; but they are very unhappy because they may falsely assume everyone else is doing better than they are. (In thinking about that statement, however, realize that you could over-simplify it. You need to remember how complex an individual really is. What it really means is that if you are low in SE **but** also have a very high need to achieve, you may actually perform better than another person who is high in SE but who has a lower need to achieve.) So,

1

you must interpret your SE within a context of many other personality factors, such as your motives, your personality traits, and the like, which are all explained more fully in this book.

The more you know and love yourself, the less likely you are to harm another. The more you accept and love your own body, the less likely you are to hurt another body.

The following true story will clearly explain the need to understand self-esteem in anyone's life — including your own. It will also show you how important an issue it is.

This is a story of exhibitionism and self-esteem. Bill was handsome, bright, sophisticated and in his early 50's. An executive, he worked as president of his own business. He came to SECS with tears running down his cheeks, explaining how desperately he needed to get over his serious problem of exhibitionism. "I'm going to lose my job, my business, all my money and my freedom. I can't bear the thought of going to jail. But I can't help myself. I have this horrible compulsion to exhibit myself all the time. I do it almost daily and frequently on weekends. You have to help me to stop. I can't stop myself."

Bill was taught to use the methods in this book. His self-esteem score initially was low. We decided not to work directly on his exhibitionism per se, at first, but to try to help him increase his own self-esteem on a daily basis, with a specific goal-setting program as outlined in this book.

Bill's perversion of exhibitionism could have been caused by more than one motivation. For example, most exhibitionists do not display their genitals to seduce a young woman into making love. Rather the intent is to shock her. If she is upset, embarrassed, angry, runs away, and especially, if she calls the police, the pervert has in his own mind the complete proof his genitals are very important.

Bill was most likely to exhibit himself following a humiliation earlier that day. We did alert him to the hostile elements he experienced in his excitement. For him, Bill's exposing his genitals served as a kind of rape or forced intrusion into the woman's sensitivities. (At least that was one way he fantasized it). If Bill could not see in her horrified expression how his behavior harmed her, the event was a failure for him. (Bill was, of course, even more humiliated by any woman who was amused, rather than shocked, at his free show. What this naturally means to women who want to discourage perverts is another matter to be discussed later.)

Therefore, you can understand why an exhibitionist displays his penis only to strange women who would be shocked, rather than a wife who would consider it too ordinary. She would not feel assaulted. Therefore, she would never respond with outrage.

Bill needed to understand the antecedents to his acts of exhibitionism. He needed to comprehend how his low self-esteem did not help him cope with rejections, humiliations and the resulting bad feelings he received at work.

Once he understood all these issues, he could work directly on increasing his self-esteem. That is precisely what Bill did. In just a very few days, as his self-esteem rose, he no longer needed to expose himself. He was quickly cured of a very bad habit that had afflicted him and his victims for years.

The SECS sex therapist did not even have to work on his exhibitionism directly.

You can begin to see the need to learn more about self-esteem. Fortunately, your own personal situation may not be as serious. But the fact remains that self-esteem is most important in all phases of a person's life: at work, at home, and at play.

Your own self-esteem is paramount in your own feelings about yourself as you look in the mirror, react to your loved ones, or interact with bosses, employees, or colleagues in any organization.

We hope this volume will help you increase your self-esteem for a more rewarding life.

Chapter 1

Increasing Your Self-Esteem

In all the people who contact SECS — Sexual Enrichment Counseling Services (Chicago) — for any reason, a glaring lack of self-esteem is obvious. The same lack of self-esteem is apparent in all patients seeking therapy from any psychologist, or other mental health professional.

To understand how your lack of, or diminished, self-esteem is related to your life, please fill out the following questionnaire. Try to answer it as quickly as possible, without thinking too much about a particular question. Usually, the first idea that enters your mind is the most correct one. Be as honest and open with yourself as you possibly can, because no one else has to know your score. (If you try to lie to yourself, you have an even bigger problem!)

Remember, whatever you score, you can always be a **winner**. Fortunately, now you can become an even **bigger** winner by doing something about it.

After you finish the questionnaire, follow the directions on how to score it.

Self-Esteem Evaluation*

Do not be concerned about your Self-Esteem score, no matter how low it may be. For your Self-Esteem simply is what it **is**, the automatic product of your heritage and total life experience; and thus nothing to be ashamed or embarrassed about. It is important, however, that you understand each statement and be completely honest with yourself in order to obtain as valid a score as possible. Furthermore, do not confuse any concepts or ideals you may hold with how you actually function. For your beginning Self-Esteem Index (SEI) is an important reference point for gauging your progress in building Self-Esteem. Remember that no matter how low your SEI may be, you can bring it up to any desired value by conscientious effort. You may also find comfort in the fact that lack of sound Self-Esteem is a universal problem that varies only in degree. It is, however, often so well camouflaged by false fronts that only a trained observer can detect it.

Score as follows: "0" If not true   "2" If largely true
                    "1" If somewhat true   "3" If true

*© 1973 by Lilburn S. Barksdale, The Barksdale Foundation, P.O. Box 187, Idyllwild, California 92349.

Score	Statement of Present Condition or Action

_____ 1. I usually feel inferior to others.

_____ 2. I normally feel warm and happy toward myself.

_____ 3. I often feel inadequate to handle new situations.

_____ 4. I usually feel warm and friendly toward all I contact.

_____ 5. I habitually condemn myself for my mistakes and shortcomings.

_____ 6. I am free of shame, blame, guilt and remorse.

_____ 7. I have a driving need to prove my worth and excellence.

_____ 8. I have great enjoyment and zest for living.

_____ 9. I am much concerned about what others think and say of me.

_____ 10. I can let others be "wrong" without attempting to correct them.

_____ 11. I have an intense need for recognition and approval.

_____ 12. I am usually free of emotional turmoil, conflict and frustration.

_____ 13. Losing normally causes me to feel resentful and "less than."

_____ 14. I usually anticipate new endeavors with quiet confidence.

_____ 15. I am prone to condemn others and often wish them punished.

_____ 16. I normally do my own thinking and make my own decisions.

_____ 17. I often defer to others on account of their ability, wealth or prestige.

_____ 18. I willingly take responsibility for the consequences of my actions.

_____ 19. I am inclined to exaggerate and lie to maintain a desired image.

_____ 20. I am free to give precedence to my own needs and desires.

_____ 21. I tend to belittle my own talents, possessions and achievements.

_____ 22. I normally speak up for my own opinions and convictions.

_____ 23. I habitually deny, alibi, justify or rationalize my mistakes and defeats.

_____ 24. I am usually poised and comfortable among strangers.

_____ 25. I am very often critical and belittling of others.

_____ 26. I am free to express love, anger, hostility, resentment, joy, etc.

_____ 27. I feel very vulnerable to others' opinions, comments and attitudes.

_____ 28. I rarely experience jealously, envy or suspicion.

_____ 29. I am a "professional people pleaser."

_____ 30. I am not prejudiced toward racial, ethnic or religious groups.

_____ 31. I am fearful of exposing my "real self."

_____ 32. I am normally friendly, considerate and generous with others.

_____ 33. I often blame others for my handicaps, problems and mistakes.

_____ 34. I rarely feel uncomfortable, lonely, and isolated when alone.

_____ 35. I am a compulsive "perfectionist."

_____ 36. I accept compliments and gifts without embarrassment or obligation.

_____ 37. I am often compulsive about eating, smoking, talking or drinking.

_____ 38. I am appreciative of others' achievements and ideas.

_____ 39. I often shun new endeavors because of fear of mistakes or failure.

_____ 40. I make and keep friends without exerting myself.

_____ 41. I am often embarrassed by the actions of my family or friends.

_____ 42. I readily admit my mistakes, shortcomings and defeats.

_____ 43. I experience a strong need to defend my acts, opinions and beliefs.

_____ 44. I take disagreement and refusal without feeling "put down," or rejected.

_____ 45. I have an intense need for confirmation and agreement.

_____ 46. I am eagerly open to new ideas and proposals.

_____ 47. I customarily judge my self-worth by personal comparison with others.

_____ 48. I am free to think any thoughts that come into my mind.

_____ 49. I frequently boast about myself, my possessions and achievements.

_____ 50. I accept my own authority and do as I, myself, see fit.

_____ **Self-Esteem Index**, i.e., your "SEI."   Date _____

To obtain your Self-Esteem Index: Add the individual scores of all **even** numbered statements (i.e. Nos., 2, 4, 6, 8, etc.). From this total subtract the sum of the individual scores of all **odd** numbered statements (i.e., Nos. 1, 3, 5, 7, etc.). This **net score** is your **current** Self-Esteem Index, or SEI. For example: if the sum of all the individual scores of the even numbered statements is 37 and the sum of all the individual scores of the odd numbered statements is 62, your SEI is 37 − 62 or a **minus** 25. The possible range of one's Self-Esteem Index is from − 75 to + 75. Experience shows that any score under + 65 is handicapping; a score of 35 or less is seriously handicapping, and a Zero or a minus score indicates a truly crippling lack of Self-Esteem.

Please do not read beyond this point until you have scored your results and double-checked them. Your score should range somewhere from a − 75 to a + 75.

In various studies that we have conducted, we discovered the mean (average) score for a typical college graduate is + 22. The mean (average) score for a typical MBA executive is a + 28.

If your score is somewhere between − 75 and + 22, you will have to work harder than someone whose score is between + 22 and + 75. But even if your score exceeds + 22, you will still feel much better about yourself by developing an action-oriented growth program, outlined in previous chapters and below here.

Try, right here and now, to outline your own program to improve your self-esteem. Please remember that you will need to raise your own level of self-esteem. There is no magic pill anyone can give you. A tranquilizer will never do it. Nor is there any magic wand that some guru can wave over your head. Only you can raise your own level of self-esteem.

It's hard work, daily, but the results will pay off one thousand fold, at least. First, your pay off will be in the way you feel about yourself. You will be giving yourself more warm fuzzies instead of cold prickly feelings. Besides these more positive feelings you will have when alone, you will receive more warm feelings whenever you relate to the people you live with. Thirdly, it will pay off for you at work in all your human relations. You will doubtlessly earn more money and get bigger and better promotions.

Here is one way to initiate a concrete, explict, definite program that you **must** become **committed** to. First, turn back and look at all the odd numbered items on the Self-Esteem Questionnaire (#1, 3, 5, 7, 9, etc.) Item

8

#9 is usually rated high for many folks with low self-esteem: "I am much concerned about what others think and say of me." Now, if you have given yourself a score of 2 or 3, it may mean this can be a problem for you.

Pete, for example, should have learned an important idea when he was young, but he never realized it until he underwent therapy: here is the idea—"you can be completely happy and successful, even if there is one dumb S.O.B. out there who doesn't like you."

Most people can become very neurotic worrying because a boss passed their desk without handing out a raise. Or, a co-worker passed you by at the water cooler without applauding you. Or, if your next door neighbor was in too big a hurry to talk. So, you have worried about it too much. O.K. Now's your chance to do something about it.

(1) **Select a goal**: For example, "From now on, I will **not** permit myself to be upset or worry because Don, my boss, snubs me at 9:00 A.M. (probably because he has bigger problems!)" You must pick a definite person, and time, and place where this usually occurs.

(2) **Record quantity and circumstances of behavior**: For example, is this person my boss more than anyone else? Or, my husband/wife, lover, parents? Where does this typically occur? You will want to determine mostly when, where and who.

(3) **Change setting events**: Try not to put yourself in those places and times recorded in step #(2) above. But, if you have to be there, then try to not let these negative thoughts, doubts, worries and/or fears take hold. Resolve to put these cold pricklies out of your mind immediately.

(4) **Establish effective consequences**: As soon as you are able to be aware of harboring these negative thoughts, and you **do** put them out of your mind, you can then give yourself a positive reinforcer, a reward. A good reward, for example, might be money (25¢, 50¢ or $1.00) in a kitty for your next new item of clothes. Or, if you catch yourself dwelling on the negative thought too morosely for too long a time, you could consciously do something distasteful, e.g., go clean a closet.

(5) **Focus on contingencies**: Make a sign or note describing the desired behavior and its consequences and place it where you will see it, e.g. on your desk, mirror, or kitchen table, and write down "I will not dwell on feelings and thoughts about what others (my boss, husband/wife, etc.) may incorrectly be thinking about me."

(6) **Achieve covert control**: Tell yourself the negative consequences of the harmful behavior to be avoided ("People who always look backwards over their shoulders can't see where they are going." "Monday morning quarterbacking every day doesn't help me do better next time."). Then, tell yourself the positive consequences of what you really want ("Greater self-confidence will help me earn more money." "Women like self-confident men more.") For some people, it is very helpful to focus on the ultimate consequences of being totally lacking in self-esteem. ("If I don't like me, neither will anyone else." "Lack of self-esteem leads to loneliness, serious depressions and suicide in the long run.")

After you have tried that growth program for some time, write yourself another one. Take item #5, for example: "I habitually condemn myself for my mistakes and shortcomings."

(1) **Select a goal**: "Stop self-blaming."

(2) **Record quantity and circumstances of behavior**: "Where, when and with whom do I usually catch myself blaming myself.? Is it everytime I say the wrong thing to a customer, or client, or patient, or child? Is it everytime I ejaculate prematurely, or don't get erect at all?

(3) **Change triggering events**: "I will not attempt to work with customers and the like when overly tired later than 8:00 p.m. after a twelve hour day. I will go home early."

(4) **Establish effective consequences:** "If I leave work before 8:00 p.m. after completing a ten or twelve hour day, I will reward myself by having a beer or cocktail. If I work too late again, I will donate money to my favorite charity."

(5) **Focus on contingencies**: "I will call attention to whatever seems to cause me to blame myself and make up a sign or note about it. The note will say: 'What causes a person to be blaming him/herself? _____ event is not sufficient to be causing me to be blaming myself'."

(6) **Achieve covert control**: Keep telling yourself that "self-blamers are no fun to do things with." Or, from the positive viewpoint, "I must love myself first before anyone else can do so." "Wanting love from others should be enough to motivate me to love rather than blame."

By now it is clear for you. You know how to make up your own action-oriented personal growth program about self-esteem. Our suggestion right here and now is for you to do exactly the same as we did for you in the two previous examples just given. Please do make up another program for yourself. Take one of the odd numbered items in the Self-Esteem Questionnaire (#1, 3, 5, 7, etc.) that seems to be a problem for you and then construct a written program about it. Just fill in the blanks.

(1) **Select a goal**: _____

_____

_____

_____

_____

(2) **Record quantity and circumstances of behavior:** _____

_____

_____

_____

_____

(3) **Change triggering events:** _____

_____

_____

_____

_____

(4) **Establish effective consequences:** _____

_____

_____

_____

_____

(5) **Focus on contingencies:** _____

_____

_____

_____

_____

(6) **Achieve covert control:** _____

_____

_____

_____

_____

Now that you have been able to measure your own level of Self-esteem, and develop programs about it, you may be wondering how we define Self-esteem.

The Barksdale Foundation of Idyllwild, California, 92349, founded by L.S. Barksdale publishes a large number of outstanding books and pamphlets on self-esteem. One of their best is *Building Self-esteem*. Here is how "Barks" describes it:

> Our basic need and urge is to "feel good" about ourselves, mentally, physically and *emotionally*. This need is responsible for our ultimate motivation. For regardless of our immediate objective, everything we do is to achieve a sense of total well-being. Unfortunately, few if indeed any of us, have sufficient awareness to know always what will make us feel

really good about *ourselves*. Herein lies our crucial need for good self-esteem. For we cannot possibly feel good and at peace with ourselves without a significant sense of adequacy and self-worth."

All our goals, hopes, and aspirations are based on this fundamental need. The more limited and distorted our awareness, the more misleading and unfulfilling are our efforts.

Please look at it this way for a moment. People smoke, take drugs, drink booze, and seek love and sex in all its phases. Other people may compulsively have needs to win, or appear better than others. We have needs to help others. We are motivated to avoid mistakes. Rich people are constantly motivated to hoard more wealth than they can ever use. Just continue to think for a moment about all the typical human motives and needs you experience in one day, especially our desperate urges to love and be loved, to be approved and accepted, and to be respected and looked up to. The ultimate motivation behind all these above mentioned urges or needs is the universal human need for "feeling good." That's the need we have to increase our self-esteem.

Self-Esteem: What Is It?

Barksdale defines self-esteem, on a subtle and often unconscious level as how one actually **feels** about oneself, based on your own individual sense of personal worth and importance. How much do you value yourself? The answer to that question is your level of self-esteem.

The main reason why it is hard to make or perform the self-esteem programs described earlier is because your present level of self-esteem is the result of your entire life's history. From our earlier childhood we have developed subtle and non-conscious feelings that have become fixed in our awareness. Thus, you have to learn to modify feelings that have become unconscious factors in your awareness.

High self-esteem principally comes from your accepting complete responsibility for your personal well being and taking complete charge of your own life. High self-esteem basically means you have to learn to accept yourself completely as an inherently valuable person, regardless of past mistakes, problems, and non-achievement of your goals.

Low self-esteem, on the other hand, can come about because of unrealistic comparisons and/or irrational beliefs about perfection. For example, you can be happy today even if you are not as rich as Rockefeller. You do not have to be comparing yourself with billionnaires. You can be a desirable woman today, even if your bosom is not as perfect as a Playmate of the Month. You need not and must not be constantly comparing yourself to others. You can be very successful today, even if you are not a president of a company. You need not be always making comparisons in every way. These ideas, then, can provide another basis for you to be making a different self-esteem growth program. Select a goal: "I will not make comparisons all day between myself and _____ or any other person(s)."

Many people have developed unconscious irrational beliefs about their need for perfection. So, you may be haunted daily by feeling that you are not **really** worthy; that you **must** or **should** be better. And, of course, you may not really know why, at a conscious level, you must be perfect.

Low self-esteem typically results from many negative feelings and negative emotional reactions that have in turn led you to feel dependent, inferior, or badly about yourself. Your parents, for example, may have repeatedly made statements to you like "children should be seen and not heard." Or, they may have said: "Mom or Dad knows best." Similar comments could have led you to feel poorly as if you are too lacking to be treated with respect. Janice was a good example of this syndrome. She came to SECS seeking orgasms, so that as she said "she might be able to escape loneliness through marriage." Her statement was very revealing. "I know my self-esteem is so low. I have never believed that I deserved pleasure, from myself or others."

Just as beauty is in the eyes of the beholder, so does your self-esteem brighten or darken your perception of your surroundings. In the same way, your self-esteem influences all your emotional responses, moods or attitudes, which includes your feelings of loneliness. If you have low self-esteem, you will tend to feel inferior, and thus have difficulty accepting a compliment. So you may suspect whoever gives you a compliment as a hypocrite or a manipulator, because you yourself **know** how bad you really, really are.

You can begin now to see the inklings of another growth program. Select a goal: "I will always accept a compliment and say "Thank you."

Your self-esteem is **not** an intellectual, cognitive idea but rather a **feeling** or a whole host of feelings deeply hidden. Most people do not even give conscious attention to their feelings of self-esteem. In fact, in one management development seminar, every executive wrote on the final, confidential evaluation form that they never once had previously given any attention to their level of self-esteem. Needless to say, many of them had very low levels of measured self-esteem.

What Self-Esteem Is Not

Sometimes, you can understand concepts better by looking at their opposites. Self-esteem is **not** a kind of egotistical self-love. On the contrary, the most obvious, crucial symptoms of people with low self-esteem is their inordinate need to boast or puff themselves up. Deep down inside you, if you have good self-esteem, you know your own self-worth and can appreciate it. But most people do not. They really need to work at it.

If you have difficulties accomplishing what has just been described here, you may need more professional help from any therapist you can trust or become more open and honest with.

Jim was a good example of a young man who disliked himself. He actually used the word "loathed." He came to SECS for therapy, stating his goals were: (1) to get over his total lack of self-confidence, (2) reduce his extreme fear of women, (3) learn how to function in bed with a woman, and finally,

13

(4) understand how to develop intimate relationships as a way to reduce severe loneliness.

For Jim, his self-esteem was not an enumeration of his abilities on an intellectual level. A person can have great talents and yet not esteem oneself. Skid row (and all of recorded history) are filled with gifted people who have succumbed to drugs, alcohol, and suicides to escape themselves. One essentially has to learn how to accept oneself on an emotional level.

Chapter 2

Risk-Taking for Greater Self-Esteem

Bill came to see a sex therapist at SECS — Sexual Enrichment Counseling Services (Chicago) — and when asked what he wanted, Bill replied: "I am horribly lonely. I have never had a date with a woman in my entire life. Loneliness is the worst way to live, and yet it is the only way I know how to live." With tears streaming down his cheeks, he quivered: "Can you please help me?"

The therapist asked what he had been doing about his problem. Bill opened a large envelope and pulled out a foot-thick computer printout, listing names and phone numbers of eager women from a dating service. Then he stated: "I am afraid to call anyone of them. I have no self-confidence."

Bill was definitely not a risk-taker. Yet, most people might admit they would like to learn to take bigger risks, to attain their goals and satisfy their needs. Risk-taking behavior is one way to "stretch" yourself to achieve personal growth goals such as developing more self-esteem. Risk-taking has been defined as behavior you would not usually engage in at this time in your life. You typically have not done a certain thing or engaged in a particular behavior you see as posing a possible threat to you. It may not appear to be a real threat to some other people, but you surely do fear it. Usually, what seems to be a risk for you is new behavior or skills you have not yet learned. In Bill's case, he had not yet learned to phone women and deal with the potential fear of rejection.

Risk-taking, then, involves a subjective sense of danger that one must learn to overcome.

Creative risk-taking can be learned. It can become an important way to increase your variety of possible responses available to you. By owning a larger repertoire of responses, you have more freedom of choice. You will not be restricted by fears or inhibitions. Your self-esteem will grow.

Then you can have greater spontaneity of action. You can become more flexible in relating to all people.

The purpose of the following questionnaire about risk-taking is to see where you are presently. Are you a risk-taker or not? Do you want to learn more risk-taking behaviors to avoid loneliness, or to obtain more love, friendship, self-esteem and the like? You can see how you compare with

15

others. You can also stimulate your thinking about risks. Hopefully, this can be discussed seriously with others who are important to you.

Please read the following statements and rank them as to how much personal subjective risk you feel might be involved. Use any reference group you prefer, such as the people you live with or work with. Put down your first answer as quickly as possible, because it will most likely be your most honest answer. Do not spend time thinking or rationalizing about it. Write the appropriate number from the scale next to each item.

Remember, whatever you score, you can always be a **winner**. Fortunately, now you can become an even **bigger winner** by doing something about it.

Risk-Taking Evaluation

Score: 0 — Would be no risk for me
1 — Would be a small risk for me
2 — Would be a moderate risk for me
3 — Would be a high risk for me

_____ 1. Disclosing certain events about my past to people.

_____ 2. Revealing definite negative feelings about myself to others.

_____ 3. Breaking out of a familiar routine.

_____ 4. Expressing anger toward anyone.

_____ 5. Getting involved with someone even though there may be rejection.

_____ 6. Showing affection toward someone.

_____ 7. Seeking help with my problems from others.

_____ 8. Starting something new (and feeling very happy about it!)

_____ 9. Receiving affection from someone.

_____ 10. Asking, rather than just wondering, if my partner **really** loves me.

_____ 11. Asking for feedback from significant members of a group.

_____ 12. Making up my mind quickly about a major life decision and sticking to it.

_____ 13. Touching someone else physically.

_____ 14. Putting up bail-bond money for my best friend without question.

_____ 15. Having someone else touch me.

_____ 16. Becoming personal and close with another in a group.

_____ 17. Risking money for the sheer excitement of gambling.

_____ 18. Making statements that might anger someone else.

_____ 19. Expressing sexual attraction for someone.

_____ 20. Typically driving too fast, swerving into and out of traffic.

_____ 21. Walking out of a group while under stress.

_____ 22. Actively betting on events, from sporting activities to politics.

_____ 23. Admitting openly that someone has hurt my feelings.

_____ 24. Telling others to leave me alone or get off my back.

_____ 25. Becoming the center of attention in a group.

_____ 26. Giving another person or group member some negative feedback.

_____ 27. After receiving money in an unexpected legacy, risking half the capital.

_____ 28. Expressing my confusion or uncertainty in the presence of others.

_____ 29. Accepting a new job for less money initially, but with better prospects for outstanding performance.

_____ 30. Expressing and handling conflicts with another individual.

_____ 31. After winning the jackpot on a fruit machine ("one-armed bandit"), feeding the coins right back in.

_____ 32. Revealing my feelings about my physical traits in a group.

_____ 33. Sharing my feelings about another's physical traits in a group.

_____ 34. Showing indifference to other members of a group.

_____ 35. Making no provisions for retirement in the early stages of work life.

_____ 36. Telling another person that he/she has become important to me.

_____ 37. Revealing a fantasy about some member or a whole group.

_____ 38. Discussing sexual feelings in a group.

_____ 39. Admitting an error I made to a group.

_____ 40. Expressing anger or dissatisfaction with a group member.

_____ 41. Admitting I feel badly for letting others down.

_____ 42. Choosing a delightful lover, even if I know it could never last.

_____ 43. Admitting I was wrong about another group member.

_____ 44. Attempting mountaineering or stock-car racing, if given a chance.

_____ 45. Risking my life for some person or cause very important to me.

_____ 46. Risking my reputation for some person or cause very important to me.

_____ 47. Risking my money for some person or cause very important to me.

_____ 48. Constantly risking new experiences in a consistent search for stimulation.

Please count up your scores now and add them up. **Do not** read further until you have a score. Remember, whatever score you have, you are a winner! But, you can improve your score and become a bigger winner, if you wish. You must put in some effort and energy to develop a growth program.

The important thing is what you really feel about yourself right here and now. If, for example, you are lonely and want more love and affection, you may begin to realize you must take risks to get what you want. All growth requires change. All change requires risk-taking.

Believe it or not, some individuals have obtained a score of zero on all 48 items. Obviously, they are big risk-takers. Others, at the opposite end of the extreme, obtained a score of 144, which means they are not risk-takers, but strong seekers of security. You should not worry about your score, but actively strive to do something about it.

Here are some possible analyses. Remember that there are definite degrees in any kind of measurement. Also, standard errors of measurement do exist. And finally, you could be some kind of exception.

Score: Under thirty. This score is very low, suggesting you are definitely a risk-taker. You may even be jeopardizing your financial, social, or domestic life. It is very likely you are involved in gambling so that your pocket suffers. Risk-taking may be fun for you, but those closest to you may judge you as reckless or foolish. Consider asking yourself why you may seem to be so fearless. You are surely not lonely for want of asking, but possibly because no one can accept it.

Score: 30-70. You may not be the world's greatest risk-taker, but you surely do take chances. As a car driver, you may be too aggressive. You may be intrigued by gambling, but respond more to the thrill of it rather than hoping to win the lottery. Some people may see you as too unreliable, or erratic. Fortunately, you may have sufficient common sense so as not to seriously hurt yourself. You may not have as much action as those who score less than 40, but you probably are not overly lonely. You might strive harder to work on your common sense. A score of 55 is average for young MBA executives in a large urban, private university.

Score: 70-100: You are not a high risk-taker, but you take chances from time to time. You may have a rather well-balanced approach in the eyes of the majority, but the high risk-taker may see you as well below average. You may see yourself, however, as moderating your normal inclination to take a chance with a healthy degree of common sense. If your better judgment advises against taking a risk, you will surely turn down the temptation.

Score: 100-120: You may be rather inhibited. You may be pretty lonely and missing out on a great amount of joy and fun. You may even be harming your career by not taking risks, even though it may seem secure on the surface. Others may reject you because you cannot make commitments to them. Then, you may be lonelier or have low self-esteem because others may want a commitment but you cannot take enough risks. You need a growth program to take more chances, somewhere, somehow, anytime.

Score: 120-144. If you have answered honestly and scored the questionnaire correctly, you are too rigid, too inflexible, and too passive. You are not any kind of a risk-taker. Others may judge you as being unable to take any chances ever. You have allowed yourself to become too handicapped. You definitely need to seek some professional help.

Risk and Change

Whether you think you are a big risk-taker, or none at all, you might consider why the topic is so very important. Everyone wants to get more out of life! In one way or another, everyone hopefully wants some growth and improvement. People cannot really be happy without growth, development, and greater self-esteem. Some of these people may falsely assume only riches or titles will make them happier. One person wants a million dollars. Another individual wants to become president. But much anecdotal evidence and research in every library suggest these are not the paths to happiness for rich people or presidents.

Growing and striving for self-actualization is what makes life worthwhile. But all growth requires change. Someone even has suggested, in the beginning, God created only continual change.

John Gardner put it well, in his excellent book, *No Easy Victories* (New York: Harper and Row, 1968, page 50). "Today, we can't afford not to take chances. I am always puzzled by people who talk as though advocates of change are just inventing ways to disturb the peace in what would otherwise be a tranquil community. We are not seeking change for the sheer fun of it. We must change to meet the challenge of altered circumstances. Change will occur whether we like it or not. It will be either change in a good and healthy direction or change in a bad and regrettable direction. There is no tranquility for us."

If lack of self-esteem, for example, is your problem, you might begin to consider this point: Opportunity is a threat to a pessimist, but a challenge to an optimist. So you could try to consider your lower self-esteem as a challenge to become more optimistic — a more optimistic risk-taker. People who are willing to be risk-takers and accept change are not typically low in self-esteem. People who are lowest in self-esteem are those who refuse any small risks.

Risk-Taking Is Personal

Risk-taking is essentially personal and subjective (idiosyncratic). Only life insurance actuaries can speak of predicting risks for large numbers of people by mathematics. The ordinary person must realize we live in a world of uncertainty that is very different for each unique individual.

Your ability to take risks, and to change through risk-taking develops from your self-concept; or, in other words, the way you perceive yourself determines how much you risk. And the way we assess ourselves differs from the ways in which others view us.

Carl Rogers has written extensively about our self-concepts (*On Becoming a Person*, Boston: Houghton-Mifflin, 1961). Most recently, in *Carl Rogers on Personal Power*, (New York: Delacorte Press, 1977), he has re-emphasized that the potential to learn and the power to act lie within the person, rather than in an expert dealing with him or her, or in a system controlling him or her. It all depends, then, on how we actively choose to look at ourselves. Karen Horney says: "For his well-functioning, man needs both the vision of possibilities, the perspective of the infinitude, and the realization of limitations, of necessities, of the concrete" (*Neurosis and Human Growth: The Struggle Toward Self-Realization*, New York: Norton, 1950). Since your self-concept is so important and so central to your personality, to increase your self-esteem, you must begin to see yourself as a risk-taker.

People may have said of you: "She's never taken a risk," or "He's a big risk-taker." When Bill first came to SECS (Sexual Enrichment Counseling Services), he stated "I wish I could do more risk-taking." But risk-taking is not really a trait like being rated somewhere on a scale, for example, from zero (very socially introverted) to one-hundred (very socially extroverted). In fact, behavioral science research has found that an extreme style of being a high or low risk-taker is usually symptomatic of a serious neurosis (N. Kogan and M. Wallach, *Risk-Taking: A Study in Cognition and Personality*, New York: Holt, Rinehart, and Winston, 1964). For a healthy person, risk-taking is viewed as an interaction of all the available alternatives, the circumstances, the resources. You can make a kind of force-field analysis that was pioneered by Kurt Lewin (see elsewhere, later).

All of Life Is a Risk

Las Vegas gamblers understand clearly that betting is risk-taking. The average person, however, often forgets that risk-taking is betting, and that you are betting every time you pass a car on a highway, buy a house or car, start up your own business, change jobs, **or even maintain things as they are Now!** Yes, maintaining the status quo is a risk.

You either bet on chance or on yourself. People do behave differently if they have a chance to affect the outcome, to become part of the equation. Your best friend may not worry about betting on a bingo game, a roll of the dice, or the talents of a mutual fund manager. In these cases, he has no direct chance to affect the results. Only the odds (luck) and another's skill affect the outcome.

Yet, other people will become bigger risk-takers if they can themselves affect the outcome; fly their plane, start up their own business, or buy their own apartment building on the fringe of a marginal neighborhood.

In these pages, we are concerned about learning not to bet on dice rolls or things outside ourselves, but learning how to bet on ourselves. Then, you can, for example, increase your self-esteem significantly.

Helen Keller is quoted: "Security is mostly a superstition. It does not exist in nature, nor do the children as a whole experience it. Avoiding danger is no safer in the long run than outright exposure. Life is either a daring adventure or nothing."

Below are some key issues for the individual who does want to learn, grow, and develop a program to become more of a risk-taker, which can help the novice or the low risk-taker to take some definite steps based on sound, logical advice. It is best to start a program where you are dealing with a relatively low risk and work your way up to tackling the greater risks after you have built up a track record of successes and failures from which you have learned.

Thirty Key Issues To Risking — Do's and Don'ts

(1) **Don't be afraid to ask questions**. You need to know as much as possible about your own life. You don't need to take an unnecessary risk because you fear asking questions. Remember, a dumb mistake is much worse than asking a dumb question.

(2) **Set goals**. You need a very clear, explicit, measurable, attainable goal so that you can tell how much you have won or lost. You need to know when to take profits or cut losses.

(3) **Consider possible losses**. If you cannot estimate a possible loss, then you don't really comprehend the risk. Don't overly complicate things by being too confused.

(4) **Don't procrastinate**. More good things are lost by procrastination than by risking. If the timing is correct and if the risk seems valuable, act quickly and decisively. After you have considered possible negative factors, work hard on the factor(s) that you can change.

(5) **Confront problems**. Don't imitate an ostrich and hide your head in the sand. Your chances will improve if you ready yourself for the problem before it sabotages you.

(6) **Accept your fears.** Playing games with yourself could be fatal. Your fears could be your alarm bells. If you ignore them at this time, the risk may still be too big for you.

(7) **Don't expect miracles**. Cleanliness may be next to Godliness, but realism is even closer. Be your own lifesaver and make your own best efforts because that's all you really have.

(8) **Bravery is for winners**. Since no one is ever 100% or 1000% successful, don't expect it. Your self-esteem would be lowered unnecessarily. Winning a small battle is better than losing a bigger war. So be brave and do it. If you lose, bravery is spelled f-o-o-l-ishness.

(9) **Invest emotion wisely**. Every emotion should be experienced and resolved directly, not indirectly through an emotional risk. If you are feeling depressed, guilty, angry, or hurt, don't resolve them through a risky act like driving too fast for road conditions. The easiest way to ruin your risks is by acting out feelings on them.

(10) **Don't exceed your limits**. Only you really know your own limits. There are no totally secure risks: that is a contradiction in terms. Rather, the only risk is in taking too many precautions. So, try to outline the circumstances under which you would take your reasonable risk.

(11) **Call "time out" for miscues**. Once you have started a risky venture, you could still goof. Just call time out, regroup your forces, and try to make any needed adjustments. Caution is changing horses after crossing the stream.

(12) **Make haste slowly.** Danger is next neighbor to security. Rehearse your risks in private. Fantasize first. Imagine what you would do, say, respond. You can reduce your fears by confronting them first in your own way, in your own mind, at your own time. Caution is thinking today and speaking tomorrow.

(13) **But don't shirk or delay**. The longer you wait, the harder it will seem. Caution is the word of cowardice for some, and what we call cowardice in others. Caution might also be called the confidential agent of selfishness.

(14) **Seek success**. Many find failure because they are not looking for success. Whenever you finally decide to take a risk, be really committed. Success is what you personally feel or think. Each person has a different meaning for and attitude toward what constitutes success. Success is the child of audacity.

(15) **Make schedules**. Timetables are not really followed by trains or planes, but **you** can at least try to make one. Any aid in prediction will make your risk easier. So will being aware of the next step.

(16) **Don't compound risks**. Too many risks mean too many results. So, don't compound your anxieties. Failing in one risk may undermine your self-confidence in another. Self esteem = pretensions/success.

(17) **Don't fight facts; adjust**. On occasion, you may have to admit the risk is too great for the realities involved. Success is outliving your sins. It is a result, not a goal.

22

(18) **Don't quit too quickly**. Success is the old ABC — ability, breaks, and courage. Jesus' definition of success was to complete one's life. It is to attain eternal life. All else is failure.

(19) **But don't hang on too long**. Just so long as to get enough to eat without being eaten.

(20) **Blame yourself only**. It is a waste of time to blame anyone else for your own failure. Save the time to start over on your next risk. Self-pity is the worst enemy.

(21) **Trust, but not too blindly**. Risking means mostly trusting yourself. If you know your blind spots — your greed, your selfishness — you can avoid the pot-holes of your inhibitions and fears. Self-trust is the essence of heroism and the first secret of success.

(22) **Risk your life only when assured of incurable cancer**. Before that time, the odds may still be in your favor. Self-preservation is the first of laws.

(23) **Seek greater self-knowledge**. Then your risks will be more self-motivated. It is hardly worth taking a risk if you do not get more self-knowledge as one result. You cannot be playing around on important issues. Self-knowledge is to be intimate at home.

(24) **Take your own risks**. You cannot afford to put your fate in another's hands. You need the experience for the time when the next bigger risk comes along that you cannot subdelegate. Self-respect is that corner-stone of all virtues.

(25) **Avoid others' risks**. You owe it to them to grow in their own ways. Trying to play the role of the protector for adults will only lead to their resenting you. In this instance, selfishness is not a true form of infantilism. Self-love is nothing more than self-affirmation.

(26) **Never risk just for the sake of proving yourself**. When we were kids, we sometimes could not estimate the danger. Since you have lived this long already, you may not want to push your luck too far. Walking a tightrope at age 72 in a gusty wind only proves something to morticians. Self-knowledge is that which grows out of man's self-confrontation with God.

(27) **List what can go wrong — and why**. Then you might be able to recognize a problem before it becomes a tragedy.

(28) **List what can go right — and why**. Then you can more readily differentiate between your assets and liabilities. Some creative problem-solving may enable you to turn a possible liability into an asset.

(29.) **Concentrate on the task**. A short-term risk will take all your energies. And your investment will pay off if you can put in enough effort, Naturally, a long-term risk will permit you to look at the other options as you go along.

(30) **Keep your ideals**. The happiest people are those who can take risks that create the best possible life for themselves. All growth is change. All change requires risks. You have to risk to grow up to be the person you want to be. Keep on truckin' once you are moving.

Risking

To laugh is to risk appearing the fool.
To weep is to risk appearing sentimental.
To reach out for another is to risk involvement.
To expose feelings is to risk exposing your true self.
To place your ideas, your dreams before the crowd is to risk their loss.
To love is to risk not being loved in return.
To live is to risk dying.
To hope is to risk despair.
To try is to risk failure.

But risks must be taken because the greatest hazard in life is to risk nothing.
The person who risks nothing, has nothing, is nothing.
He may avoid suffering and sorrow, but, he simply cannot learn, feel,
                change, grow, love . . . live.
Chained by his certitudes, he is a slave;
He has forfeited his freedoms.
Only a person who risks is free.

Chapter 3

Power Through Imagery

William Shakespeare said "Imagination, my mind's eye." This is surely one of your greatest strengths for increasing your feelings of self-esteem. You could profit much from using this great power, which most people either do not understand, or else overlook.

Pictures you develop in your own mind just like a Polaroid camera become self-fulfilling prophecies.

If you imagine yourself unable to handle problems, you are doomed to be victimized by them. On the other hand, if you typically picture yourself becoming more successful, attaining goals in definite areas of your life, you can make the transition from imagination to reality.

In a step-by-step manner, you can direct your imagination and willpower to change and grow. By a system of exercises, you can reshape your life to become closer to whatever you want to be.

There is a vast power in mental imagery. You can learn how to tap into it and harness this energy. This fantastic power of imagery can be used in solving many kinds of problems. Here you can learn how to apply it in your own life so that you can have greater self-esteem.

The dictionary defines imagery as a "picture in your mind of something not actually present."

Suppose, for example, that I ask you to describe your mother. You would close your eyes for a while and then give your answer. To describe the various features of your mother, or any person not present, you would have to visualize the person in your mind's eye. It is the process of building an image-picture or an imagination-portrait.

Psychologists have long taught us that everyone has these images in their heads, regardless of whatever other diverse thinking, problem-solving, or wishing is pervading their minds. Just relax now and close your eyes. You will focus on some imaginary pictures. Imagination has been defined as the "eyes of the soul."

First you may need to strengthen your powers of imagery. These powers usually lie below your levels of awareness. Some theorists have long believed our "unconscious" or "subconscious" minds are like mines or whirlpools of volcanic activity below the surface, governing many of our feelings and actions. They believe we are all pawns of deeply repressed urges and mysterious impulses that ultimately influence our actions. Authorities who believe these tenets seldom see things as they truly exist. For them, all personal interaction is symbolic of more fundamental issues. For example, they view creativity as sexual sublimation; ambition as overly compensated insecurity.

One reason why theorists interpret human behavior in such complex and mysterious ways is clear: we are problem-solvers fascinated by complex rather than simple phenomena.

Yet, recent research reveals many uncomplicated results about human beings. We all think on verbal and nonverbal levels. When meditating on important issues, a vast panoply of pictures and images always accompanies and feeds into our feelings.

Here is how you can test it for yourself now.

Concentrate on whatever makes you feel especially joyful. Consider those people, or situations that make you feel good, happy, joyful and content. Remember it now. Put down this book momentarily, taking your time.

Next, focus on events and situations that make you feel depressed or sad. What causes you to feel disconsolate, upset, sorrowful? Again, put down this book and momentarily think about it.

For a third example, concentrate on whatever makes you feel angry. What causes you to feel mad, hostile, or enraged? Again, put down this book and momentarily dwell on it.

Finally, imagine what makes you feel fearful. What stimuli make you feel anxious, worrying, downright scared? Again, momentarily put down this book and think about it.

Now, consider what was happening in your mind's eye as you had these experiences. Did you just think in words? Or, rather, did various images and photographs run through your mind, as if you were watching a TV set in your home? As you read this now, you can experience in your own mind whatever movies you choose, the series of mental images called forth by significant feelings and emotions.

Despite this awareness, many people downplay or do not accept the powers of their mental imagery. They do not understand how mental images can **cause** emotional problems. Yet imagery unleashes the most potent personality forces to overcome daily stresses.

Idealized Self-Image

Another method to increase your self-esteem has been called the ISI — idealized self-image — by Dr. Dorothy Susskind of Hunter College at the City University of New York. (John Keats said: "What the imagination seizes . . . must be truth — whether it existed before or not.")

Implementing the ISI includes these steps:

(1) After you relax as well and as comfortably as you can, close your eyes. Imagine yourself with certain traits and abilities that you would like to possess. Picture yourself achieving certain qualities

that can be attained in a brief time period, rather than an impossibly nebulous ISI. Do not imagine yourself as rich as Rockefeller, or just "successful." You must be more specific, such as picturing yourself "relating better to a certain blonde or a tall, dark, handsome man," or "a boss at 9:00 a.m." Try imagining yourself developing more sophistication at a party, or on the job, as you approach someone to introduce yourself.

(2) In your own imagination, compare your present, real self-concept with your ISI. This step will enable you to determine goals to work on for the new ways you want to act.

(3) Increasing your self-esteem, in part, requires you to remember what you did well in the past. Concentrate on that event, intensely and continuously until you conjure up again all your feelings of accomplishment and achievement. Relish them often, every day.

(4) Apply those feelings of accomplishment to your present and future behaviors. It is just as easy to think positively and optimistically about your activities as it is to feel negatively about them, and infinitely more rewarding.

(5) Continuously concentrate on your ISI. Identify with your ISI whenever you do anything like going to work, looking at yourself in the mirror while combing your hair or whatever.

(6) Act as your ISI would behave at all times. If you discover any divergence between the way you presently act and your ISI, determine what is happening. Try to remedy that interference and turn your spotlight back on your ISI.

If you dwell on your mistakes, rejections or inadequacies, you can expect to fail. Your faulty self-image will become a negative self-fulfilling prophecy. Focusing on your new, positive ISI will change self-defeating behaviors into optimistic, constructive activities that increase your self-esteem.

John Ruskin said "imagination is reaching, by intuition and intensity of gaze ...a more essential truth than is seen at the surface of things." George Bernard Shaw called "imagination the beginning of creation. You imagine what you desire; you will what you imagine; and at last you create what you will."

Role-Taking Imagery

TV has been called one of our country's biggest addictions. Football widows will be among the first to attest to that point. TV and movie viewing is one of the most obvious, explicit forms of imagery. If you are ever tempted to assume you have no powers of imagination, just consider how well you imagine as you view movies or TV.

You can use this great skill to enhance your self-esteem for all phases of your life, whether to get a better job, improve your social/sexual life, or decrease your loneliness. Albert Einstein said imagination is more important than knowledge.

The basic idea is simple: **If you seriously and consistently imagine yourself achieving a goal, your chances of real success will be definitely improved.**

Frequently, to achieve this success you can use the method of exaggerated role-taking, first emphasized by psychologist, Arnold Lazarus in 1966. Since you learn many things in life by imitating those whom you admire, exagerrated role-taking is just another example. You simply imagine someone else easily accomplishing whatever you wish to do yourself. Basically, you imagine, then imitate, and finally continually imagine yourself imitating to a greater degree.

Suppose you have an employee who irritates you and you constantly blow up. As an example, a boss mentioned she was always losing her temper at a secretary. Whenever the young woman misbehaved, the boss would become tense, over-react, and vociferously attack. The secretary would cry. The boss was overcome by guilt. "How can I stop?" she wondered. "I promised myself thousands of times to treat employees differently."

Exaggerated role-taking helped her. First the boss outlined the behavior traits she wished to emulate. Next, she was asked to imagine someone who exemplified these qualities. She had a colleague whom she considered self-confident, laid back, graceful and elegant. The boss was encouraged, when the employee next goofed, to imagine her controlled, gracious friend. Would she scream? Of course not! Would she lose her temper? No, never! You can see how you would act in your mind's eye and **then imitate her**. She discovered, and so can you, how imitation and exaggerated role-assuming improved her self-control and also her self-confidence.

You can practice situations just described well in advance of the actual event. Thus, the boss while relaxing at home, can see the employee misbehaving and can imagine herself or the ideal boss responding in a positive, constructive fashion.

There are, naturally, different degrees of exaggeration. For instance, a rather ordinary, anxious, shy, young man who was overwhelmed about dating was encouraged to imagine he was actually a prince in disguise who had agreed to date a commoner. He was to clarify this picture in his own mind and continually assert to himself: "I am a prince, you are a commoner." Because of his active imagination, he was able to overcome his fears quickly. Then, he dropped the role and was his normal self, finally having a good time.

Many applications of this method can be found daily. Imaginary role-assuming is especially useful whenever you are with people who make you feel nervous, or lacking in self-confidence. Employees who feel fearful of bosses are natural candidates for this technique.

Remember, the heart of the role-assuming method is to convince yourself what would be your best response in a situation. You can conclude this by discussing it with friends, bosses, lovers or if need be, a therapist.

Then, after relaxing, you clearly imagine yourself engaging in the behavior you desire. You can choose to add the exaggeration part of it to feel even more self-confident. One successful young woman had to relate to chauvinistic men at a production meeting. If she imagined herself owning a secret weapon that could eliminate them all, she instantly felt self-confident. Then she could respond in the assertive way that she practiced daily in her imagery exercises.

Imagination on the Job

Job interviews are prime examples where people need to rehearse and imagine how they will function. An entire volume about how to accomplish this method more effectively in advancing your career has been written. (Dean C. Dauw: *Up Your Career!, 3/E.* Waveland Press, Inc.: Prospect Heights, Illinois). You can avoid nebulous wishing and spend more time imagining how well you will perform. Picture an explicit scene in your mind's eye. Use many different pictures. In one of them, focus on meeting the interviewer. Visualize yourself taking the initiative, and convincing her why you would be the best person for the job. Rehearse questions she might ask you and fantasize brilliant answers affirming all your good traits and abilities. Sell yourself in front of your mirror at home. Imagine being very self-assured. As clearly as possible, see yourself sitting, walking, conversing in a very self-confident fashion. The more you practice these images, the more chances they will affect your interviews.

Another obvious application of imagery on the job involves sales people, as in high-pressure fields like life insurance, securities or real estate. Sales success results from rehearsing every possible event in your own mind, at your own leisure. A young MBA client was fired from a management job in a bank. Disconsolate, he cried in the counselor's office. Eventually, using methods described in *Up Your Career!*, he was able to choose a new career in sales. He imagined every day becoming the most successful young salesman in his field. A few months later, he called me to announce he had sold a million-dollar account. Remember, you significantly increase your chances of success by constantly imagining yourself accomplishing your goal.

Behavior and Goal Rehearsal

Goal rehearsal is a more explicit example of what was described above in imaginary role-taking and imagery on the job. It's another step on the ladder to the fourth dimension.

Do not let this objection obstruct you. Those who ascribe great value to spontaneity and creativity may be upset at the idea of preparing a script. Since everyone does not have a rapier wit or matchless repartee, many people need to rehearse a goal. Otherwise, by relying too much on spontaneity, they would improvise themselves into a dead-end. A challenging phone call can often be made more successful by planning in advance.

In fact, many people do not plan far enough in advance. Countless inter-personal situations could be helped by goal rehearsal. You have to take in imaginary conversation as far as it will go. For instance, one man suffering through a divorce was expecting a phone call from his wife and her attorney. He tried to imagine how the discussion would progress. He rehearsed in a certain way, insisting on various rights. But he failed to plan for all possible different directions in the conversation, falsely assuming all would go his way. But it did not. The result was disastrous, because he could not counter all the new issues raised. He felt very cheated and depressed. He need not have been out-maneuvered, if he had rehearsed his goals more effectively, preparing other possible scripts.

Sexual Enrichment and Self-Confidence

My colleagues and I have conducted research at Sexual Enrichment Counseling Services — SECS — "pronounced sex" on the relationship between sexual dysfunctions and self-esteem. There is a high correlation. Most people who want to enrich their sex lives by overcoming a sexual problem have a lowered level of self-esteem. Most of our clients and research subjects were not aware of how low their level of self-esteem was. We had to teach them how to use their imagination in a better way to enhance self-esteem.

A pre-orgasmic woman, for example, can be greatly assisted by goal rehearsal. In her "homefun" assignment (after all, it's not really "homework"), she needs to consciously learn how to relax. Then, she needs to imagine herself happily, successfully, and enjoyably engaged in her sexual activities. If you can learn to imagine yourself passionately and pleasurably involved in sexual experiences, you can make a positive transfer to the real event.

This method is especially needed by men experiencing impotence. Fre-quently, these individuals are also too shy and non-assertive to ask a woman for a date in the first place. They need to imagine themselves successfully approaching a woman and asking her for a date. If that initially seems too challenging or problematical, they need to step back and begin at whatever stage seems too difficult. Joe needed to begin by imagining himself saying hello to a waitress every day before he could muster sufficient self-confidence to do it.

Then by successive approximations, he could continue imagining each step of the way. After some time at this level, he was able to progress further to engaging in a minor conversation. Later, he progressed to asking a young woman to have a cup of coffee. Eventually, Joe reached the point, through his active imagining, where he could ask for a date.

Men can rehearse scenes in which they view themselves involved in erotic experiences. If they can learn to do that, focusing on their partners rather than their own erections, then they can transfer this training to any real life situation.

Jason was another example of a man with a sexual problem that was helped by these methods. Sado-masochism was his thing. He could only achieve erections and orgasms by the obsessive sexual fantasy of a nude woman chained to a dungeon wall, begging him to loosen her. He had been masturbating with this sadistic fantasy for 15 years. He seemed eager to change that part of his sex life. He wanted to become excited by women in more typical ways.

The basic finding is: **If you want to achieve something in reality, you must first imagine yourself accomplishing it in your own mind.** Sexual potency will doubtlessly continue to remain a major area of concern for most men. So, in summary, remember: (1) You need to practice your goal rehearsal when you are not aroused. (2) You need to relax. (3) You should focus on experiences in which you view yourself performing as well as you desire. (4) You need to picture yourself with no difficulties. (5) You will want to practice these four previous steps, enhancing your imagination and increasing your self-esteem every day.

Chapter 4

Expand Your Self-Awareness

Jack is a good example of a young man who could not find a lover. He admitted he had no self-confidence. But he did not understand why his lack of self-esteem meant he could not find a woman or develop a relationship with her.

Jack had no self-awareness. Fortunately, you can absolutely increase your own self-esteem by expanding your level of awareness. When you develop a better, more accurate picture of yourself, you increase your self-esteem. This book is not directly about awareness. But you need to understand what awareness means to increase your self-esteem.

Your awareness is primarily made up of your sensing, feeling, thinking, intentions and actions.

(Each part of your awareness will be explained more completely later in this chapter.)

As you understand your own awareness better, you will become convinced **you** are **the authority** on your own awareness. You will then become aware of your **own uniqueness**. Your uniqueness is very valuable.

No one in the universe is exactly like you. At this very moment, you are the only person in the world who is sensing, thinking, feeling, wanting and behaving as you are right now.

That statement will always be true. Therefore, your uniqueness will always be true. Someone else could dress like you. A second person may have a hairdo similar to yours. A third person may even smile a little bit like you. But no one — absolutely no one — sees the world, or feels like you.

Great fortunes are spent collecting rare gems, coins and stamps. But no one is as priceless, unique or rare as you. You must learn to believe that statement and act upon it.

What is this awareness? Basically, you can imagine it as a kind of **Awareness Circle.**

The awareness circle can be viewed as a kind of pie-shaped circle involving five elements.

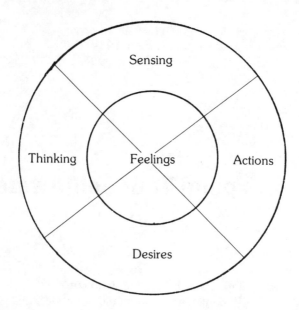

Feelings are placed in the middle because your emotions are more directly related to every other element (e.g., related to actions), and are somewhat involved in each. Consider this example: you **see** (sensing) a spectacular sunset and **feel** a rush of joy. Or, a man sees a gorgeous blonde and **feels** a rush of lust.

Naturally, your senses, feelings, ideas, desires and actions are always within you, but may not be *within* your awareness. Or, they may be only partially, to a minor degree, within your awareness.

"Self-Awareness" means becoming attuned to all these dimensions; knowing yourself better.

You will not necessarily ever achieve total, continual self-awareness of all elements simultaneously. It might be an illusory goal. But it is worth striving for, because whatever you achieve will be more rewarding than your present level of awareness, and will contribute to your greater self-esteem. Now, look at each of the five parts of your awareness wheel separately and understand what they mean.

Interpretations-Thoughts

Many people may be aware of exactly what they are thinking. Here are some other words commonly used to express your interpretations or thoughts:

Evaluations   Reasons
Assumptions   Stereotypes
Beliefs   Expectations
Conclusions   Opinions
Impressions   Ideas

Interpretations are really just all the variety of meanings you assign in your own mind to comprehend yourself, situations and others.

The most important point to consider in understanding your interpretations is that they are puzzled together by your past, present and expected experiences. And since you construct your interpretations, they will always be different from another's.

Imagine a beautiful lady walking down the avenue, smiling. Each beholder would interpret her behavior differently.

"She's appreciating the sunshine."

"She's ecstatic because she just got a raise and a promotion."

"She just finished her MBA degree."

"She's overwhelmed by a marriage proposal."

These interpretations you construct in your own mind come from the information your senses give you, the beliefs you already hold, as well as all the immediate wants, desires and feelings about the present situation.

For example, if you do not notice your partner's smile and warm voice (sense data) accompanying "You nutty person!" you could falsely conclude you're being dumped on (interpretation). This could occur more easily if you do not see the smile because you already **feel** depressed.

Examples like the previous one are unlimited. It all depends. Your interpretations depend on which sensing-information you experience, how you are feeling and what you want. But that's not all!

Your interpretations are also influenced by the thoughts you **already** harbor; by your past beliefs and assumptions. In the previous example, if you **believe** partners could lovingly and humorously name-call, you could take the remark "*You Nut!*" to mean love and affection. But, if you first **assume** your partner is angry at you, you would interpret the comment differently.

Expectations are also clear examples of how past interpretations affect your next interpretations. Sometimes your beliefs — expectations unwittingly cause behaviors completely inappropriate for your immediate objectives. Suzi really wanted to play tennis with Dan, but expected him **not** to want to go because he looked exhausted. So, she said in a doubtful tone: "You wouldn't want to play tennis, would you?" Dan retorted, "No, not tonight." Later, Dan wondered why he had declined, because he really wanted to play tennis.

A crucial point is this: your interpretations are not founded on a **real world** out there. They are built on what you perceive (sensing) plus all the feelings, intentions and prior interpretations you made. Thus, it is natural that two people could have completely different interpretations of the same data. (Every husband and wife eventually sees that, usually when it is too late!)

Your Sensing

If you can increasingly become more attuned to all your sensory input, you will become more aware, and then develop greater self-esteem. Your senses record raw data, but you then add on all kinds of interpretations. It just happens. You don't want to stop it either, because you need to make sense out of your world.

In one experiment, partners were invited to report whatever sense data they observed about each other. They were specifically told to omit feelings, interpretations, intentions and the like. They were to stick **only** to the sensory information. The results were surprising.

"You appear ecstatic." (Ecstatic is an interpretation. What sensory data suggest ecstasy? A broad smile, relaxed jaw muscles, twinkling eyes, etc.).

"I observe your nervous foot movements." (Again, nervous is an interpretation, because foot movements are raw sensory input.)

"I think you have a great amount of energy." (Clarify the data: posture, body movements, etc.).

Remember, interpretations are unavoidable. In these examples they may even have been correct. But it is necessary to separate sensory data from interpretations because they may be incongruent. You do not want to get caught in the trap of believing what you think or expect really exists — that your interpretation is really the correct one.

Your Feelings

Your emotions are your spontaneous reactions to all the expectations you have and interpretations you make. Your feelings are inside you, but have outward signs, such as blushing, tensed-up muscles, loud voice and the like. The most common examples are: sadness inside, tears outside; joy inside, smile outside.

Most people, experiments show, cannot even name some of their feelings.

Below is just a partial list of some feelings you may experience:

Courageous	Surprised
Afraid	Reluctant
Joyful	Silly
Loved	Uneasy
Satisfied	Ecstatic
Calm	Lonely
Comfortable	Excited
Pleased	Confused
Self-assured	Proud
Cautious	Gloomy
Content	Hopeful
Grief	Indifferent
Happy	Solemn
Angry	Anxious
Tired	Hate
Eager	Discontent

Your feelings are really you. They serve many functions.

1. First, your emotions can function as a barometer. As early warning signals, they help you understand your responses to events.

2. Feelings help you clarify your expectations. Many emotions are felt precisely because of the difference between what you expected and what you experienced. If, for example, you expect to be rejected, but instead you are warmly accepted, by another person, you experience surprise, joy, and excitement. If, on the other hand, you anticipate acceptance but receive rejection, you may feel very angry. You begin to understand, then, how discrepancies in expectations lead to positive or negative feelings. Your feelings can only serve these functions if you allow them into your awareness.

(Remember, in these pages, the emphasis is continually on getting in touch with all of yourself — your **own** feelings, senses, thoughts, intentions, and actions — for very important reasons that will be more completely explained soon.)

You must, therefore, give yourself permission to really become aware of your feelings rather than deny or repress them. Believe it: most people you know avoid their feelings. The most common cases are those people who deny negative feelings. For example, Betty denies her anger about her husband's premature ejaculations. She believes his problem leads to her own lack of orgasms. Bill's climaxing too quickly does not keep Betty from masturbating to orgasm, but that is a different issue. Surely, Bill's apparent unwillingness to solve his problem angers Betty. It is easier to deny those negative feelings than for Betty to admit her greater positive feelings of love for him.

Betty's situation, then, leads her to strong feelings of ambivalence (love versus hate) which she does not even recognize, so that it becomes even impossible to admit and accept them.

You can see how Betty and possibly you deny positive feelings sometimes. Why? Because it is often not convenient nor comfortable to admit and experience how important your lover/partner may be to you; the warm feelings that arise from being with him or her, and how much you care.

Here is one way to bring your own, unique feelings into your awareness. Watch for certain signs. First, there are all the obvious physical signs such as more sweating, greater heartbeats, lightheaded-floating-dizzy feelings and the like. Second, there are behavioral signals that reveal your true feelings: become quiet, laugh, avoid eye contact, cross your legs. Third, there are more indirect signals, such as when you feel gratitude, you purchase someone a gift. Joe could not express anger over his own impotence, so he called Sara stupid.

You cannot control your feelings by ignoring them. Nor does denying feelings get rid of them. But you may and can change your feelings as you permit yourself to look again at your new, incoming sense data and the old assumptions you lay on them. That is why you must learn to become more aware of all the components of your awareness-circle mentioned before.

You can experience new feelings by reconsidering your expectations, and interpretations that may in reality be misinterpretations. Mary was angry at Tom because he did not want to celebrate her promotion by going out on Friday night. He preferred to wait until Saturday or Sunday. Mary really felt disappointed and frustrated because it appeared obvious at first to her that Tom was not sufficiently excited by her good feelings and did not deserve an immediate Song and Dance from him. Then, her increasingly greater awareness revealed how exhausted Tom looked; how it was 102 degrees in the auto shop where he worked that day; how busy it was for both of them all week. Because Mary looked again at her sense data (102 degrees and Tom's drooping eyes), her assumptions, expectations, and the like, she was able to understand his desire to postpone was not an affront to her. They both felt better and Mary's self-esteem increased. She did not feel put down. She experienced where Tom's feelings were: dead tired.

Mary could have let experiences like this lead her to a constant expectation of being put-down. That is one way people develop feelings of lowered self-esteem. You may begin to understand better now how sense data, expectations and feelings interact.

On other occasions, it may be helpful to "go with" whatever you are feeling. Just permit yourself to feel it more, immerse yourself in it and let it happen. If you feel like crying, let your sorrow amplify and get out your Kleenex. Don't try to put a lid on it, or try to change it. You can't consciously change sorrow into joy by immediately snapping your fingers. This method is easier if you are happy — just let yourself fly higher. Your feelings will all have a natural flow like a river entering the ocean — one way when the tide is out and the other as the tide comes in. Your goal is not to become a Bay of Fundy where there may be a 30' difference. Give yourself permission to experience your own unique feelings and your self-esteem will rise.

Remember, you cannot control feelings by denying them or not acknowledging them. Rather, if you attempt to deny them, they will control you. Your feelings are as natural as a sunset. Accept them as yours, as a part of you. You need not explain, justify or rationalize your feelings. Just tune in to their rock and roll and accept what they are telling you about yourself. Your self-esteem will increase.

One difficult thing about feelings is that you frequently "feel" in combination. Your single feeling of love at the sight of someone may be easy to recognize simply as love. On another occasion, you may feel a combination of frustration, irritation, confusion and exhaustion. When someone asks how you are feeling, it is difficult to sort out.

To help complicate matters, the intensity of your feelings will vary. You may be very irritated, fairly irritated, mildly irritated and sometimes almost irritated.

Finally, your combination of feelings may be in conflict. This may lead you to conflicting information. Consider this example.

One evening, Marty was waiting for Kim. As it got later and later, he began to form a series of interpretations and experience various feelings:

Anger that she may have forgotten.

Concern that she may have had a car accident.

Regret that he may not have communicated more clearly about the meeting place.

When Kim finally arrived, she asked: "Are you angry?". Marty replied: "Angry? I'm furious! But I'm also elated to see you, because I was concerned and fearful of an accident. You know I also don't like to wait."

Even though your feelings may be complicated or in conflict, you need to try to spotlight them and express them. This will be discussed more later.

Your Intentions

Intention usually means moving toward or away from something or someone. For a pervert, it may be another word signifying lust. For a housewife, it may mean she is going grocery shopping. Here we use it to refer not to your long-range goals but your more immediate desires, which are usually more difficult to become aware of.

You may frequently confuse your own intentions with what you really want others to do. When this occurs, your intentions for others often surface in the form of questions or demands. The "I want" is not explicitly spoken. You may say to others:

"Would you like to go to bed with me?" rather than "I would like to go to bed with you."

"You should not do that," rather than "I want you to please not do that."

"Would you like to go to a play with me?" rather than, "I'd like to go to a play with you."

You need to learn to express your own wants more directly. Here are some of the intentions you may have:

To compromise	To be open	To be caring
To avoid	To insist	To accept
To clarify	To understand	To share
To explain	To support	To disregard
To be humorous	To meditate	To listen
To influence	To be honest	To be responsive
To assist	To hurt	To be curious
To reject	To praise	To have fun
To approach	To defend oneself	To conceal

Basically, the number of your intentions is almost limitless.

Problems arise when your intentions become "hidden agenda." This occurs when (1) you are not aware of all your intentions on occasion; (2) or you are aware but do not consider them sufficiently important to disclose to your partner; or (3) you freely decide to keep them secret.

39

Clearly, you may not choose to disclose to an insecure boss that you feel angry at him, especially if you do not have the insurance policy of a better job offer in your back pocket. Or you may feel too embarrassed to admit openly to someone that you want her to feel better about herself.

People do not reveal their true intentions to others frequently enough. You may have developed this bad habit because you did not see the importance. It may be keeping you from receiving more love, affection, attention or other good things you want. For example, why should you expect someone can read your mind. If you feel positively toward someone, you can freely choose to express your intentions toward that person. You need to accept your own desires as important to yourself and then your partner will do the same. Finally, then, your self-esteem will increase.

Phil was afraid to express his **feelings** of attraction to his girl friend, Margaret, and was even more fearful of expressing his desire to go to bed with her. Margaret really wanted to marry Phil but did not want to seduce him first for fear of being rejected. So they unfortunately drifted slowly apart, because neither person could express both feelings and intentions. Both became bigger losers by not expressing what they wanted. Both lowered their own self-esteem in the process.

Your intentions are of great importance and power because they have such a great effect on all your actions. Changing your behavior really means you must first change your desires. You may be able to "fake" your own actions to an extent, but you will find it harder to fake your own intentions to yourself, unless you are really "crazy-schizy." You mostly know whatever you want, from a martini to a steak to lovemaking. You may take a new date out for dinner, knowing you want sex but she only wants dinner; companionship now, and perhaps she wants marriage later. But she does not want sex now. Are you willing to run the risk of offending her or possibly losing her by verbalizing your true intentions?

Only you really know what you want, because your intentions are inside you. Nobody can read your mind. Therefore, honesty to yourself is intimately connected to your intentions. Both are connected to your own self-esteem. First you must find out what it is you want. Then you must honestly admit it to yourself. Then you must become aware how your self-honesty and your self-intentions are the basis for increasing your self-esteem. "**Don't Lie**" is a firm foundation for self-esteem. "Don't lie" is synonymous with increasing self-esteem.

You may intend to improve and develop your relationship with someone close to you. If you will take the risk of revealing your true intentions to your partner, your own self-esteem and your partner's will grow.

For some people it is helpful to view your intentions as secretaries organizing and planning your day. You can use them to assist you in looking at alternative actions, things you may **want** or **not want** to do. Imagine, for example, you **want** your partner to love you more and be more satisfied with you. After you spotlight that intention, you can more easily focus on possible behaviors to support that intention:

Offer to do some household chore your partner typically does.

Listen more carefully to your loved one.

Do something extra-considerate, like buying her flowers.

You may naturally not want to be always psychoanalyzing your intentions. You don't want to become an overly rational computer/robot. But whenever you are feeling especially depressed or dissatisfied or something special is happening, you may want to figure out **what you really want**: Your intentions will help you clarify what is happening.

The following are a few easy ways to help you maintain or increase your awareness of your intentions. First, you can look at the "action" dimension of your awareness circle. Trust your behavior. If you **do** something, it is possible you **wanted** to do it or at least **wanted** something related to it. Accept your actions. Usually, your behavior will tell you what you have been wanting.

A second way is to consider what your feelings reveal about your intentions. Whenever you feel satisfied or positive, your intentions are matching your behavior. Whenever you feel unhappy or dissatisfied, it usually means your more important intentions are not in sync with your actions.

A third method to identify your intentions is to meditate on some things you admit to yourself but not to others. As explained above, it is hard to lie to yourself. And you may want to avoid being phony to yourself, as many people do. Clearly look at only those things you will admit to yourself.

Like your feelings, intentions may occur singly, but frequently you want more than one thing at a time, like fish and chips, or steak and ale. "I want us to have a fun vacation. I want you to like me. I want us to feel closer to each other."

Unfortunately, intentions can often be in conflict. Conflicting intentions can lead to more confusing actions, unless you keep close watch on them. "I want to be with you now, but part of me wants to be all by myself."

Or, you may become aware of conflicts between your long-range and short-range goals. "I want to do well on my job early tomorrow but I still want to go out swinging tonight."

You may also experience conflict between two long-range intentions. "I want to try out new fun things on a different vacation, but I don't want to go to too many places."

Finally, these examples can show you how conflicting intentions, just like your conflicting feelings, can be expressed more easily when you can spotlight them.

Your Actions

The fifth and final part of your Awareness Circle is your behavior. You may believe you know what you are doing, but your actions may not always enter your awareness.

Your alert partner may be more aware of your behavior on occasion than you are. For example, you may be so tense in a certain situation that you reach for a cigarette as a way of punctuating or interrupting a conversation. Many books have recently been written on Body Language and Manwatching to prove how your facial expressions, positive and the like, reveal more than you may be presently aware of right here and now, mostly because you may be feeling anxious or whatever.

Because so much is always going on at one time, it is naturally hard for you to be aware of all your actions.

Greg and Carol were enjoying some of her new rock tapes. She rolled over and asked him: "How do you feel about this one?" Greg paused: "O.K. I like it." Carol rejoined: "Your voice doesn't sound enthusiastic." Greg got up and stared out the window. Finally, he muttered, "I think I like it." Greg was really not aware of his behavior, but his actions spoke more loudly to Carol than his words.

Your spontaneity can often be inhibited, if you are always aware of your actions. You don't want to lose any fun, but your actions are important to you for your personal debriefing.

You will want to look at patterns, such as why do you always get drunk on Friday night? By becoming aware of what you are really doing, you enhance the richness of your life. These heightened experiences will make you feel better about yourself and increase your self-esteem.

Learning to Use Your Awareness Circle

Here is one example of how to use your awareness circle.

"I observe you sitting there quietly smoking pot (sensing), and I think you must be very relaxed and content (interpreting). I feel very pleased (feeling) and I want to leave you alone so you can enjoy the experience (intention). So, I leave you alone (action)."

You will want to move step-by-step through your Awareness Circle. In your daily reality, however, it may begin with feelings.

"I'm ecstatic tonight" (feeling). He grabs her and playfully twirls her around (action). "It must be because I just got a raise and a promotion" (interpretation). "When I hear you giggling like this" (sensing), I think you're beautiful" (interpretation). "I really want to make love now" (intending).

Please put this book down now and tune into your Awareness Circle. Flow into and through each phase/part of the experience. What happens first? Your thoughts? Your feelings? Your senses? Whatever you desire? Your behavior? You may be more in touch with one part of your Awareness Circle than others.

Mike was more of a "sensation" person. "God, look at all the fans here today at the ball park" (senses). "I'm uncomfortable" (feelings). "It's too crowded" (interpretation). "I'm leaving" (intention). He exits (action).

Cathy typically experienced her feeling dimensions first. "I really dig it here. It feels so open and free." Then, she usually moved to her intentions. "I want to stay here and drink it all in; absorb it." Then she began interpreting.

"I think this is a wonderful place." Finally, she would become more aware of the sensory data. "The lake is blue, the birds are chirping and the wind smells clean."

Do you want to understand your pattern? What is your partner's? How does it differ from yours? Few partners have the same pattern, which is one reason they were attracted to one another. Try to know yours and accept your partner's. In the process, your self-esteem will rise.

Why Use the Awareness Circle?

First, it will help you know yourself better, and all the diverse dimensions and combinations of dimensions that make you the unique person you are. By giving you more information, you can think through each situation better and become more integrated. You can become more in tune with your creative uniqueness, at any moment, for your personal growth and development toward greater self-esteem.

A second major benefit is that it enhances your range of choices. The Awareness Circle information gives you more actual options, like where you are really coming from. Then, your choices are not determined by some old, bad habit, but can become more rewarding and growth inducing. If you are only coming from a kind of retarded awareness, you can have misunderstandings, more conflicts and less effective behavior.

A third good reason to use your Awareness Circle is that it improves your relationship with your partner, your boss, or friends. You can only communicate what you are aware of. By adding to the information available about yourself, you own a greater range of options to communicate. Your intended communications are limited by the level of your self-awareness. The awareness circle can expand your wider range of options that you can then freely choose to become more open about and more honest to your partner.

All our research findings suggest your increased self-awareness will give you greater self-esteem and self-confidence. The clearest information about your feelings, senses, thoughts, intentions and actions will guarantee greater awareness of your own uniqueness. Only you are the authority on your awareness. Your unique awareness is valid and valuable. No one else in the universe is like you. At this moment or at any given time, only you are feeling, sensing, thinking, wanting and acting as you are now. Your precious uniqueness is invaluable, rarer than precious gems. Only one of you exists.

Flow with your experience, and enhance your awareness. Accept it. Affirm it. Use it. In the process, you will increase your self-esteem.

Chapter 5

Self-Hypnotism to Increase Your Self-Esteem

"One picture is worth a thousand words" — old Chinese Proverb

A vast amount of evidence exists showing it is not enough to state: "I will be confident. I want a higher level of self-esteem." The words must be accompanied by a picture of yourself as the confident person you want to become.

Rochelle, a client, said to me, "I can't visualize myself as a confident person because I've never really been that way." Fortunately, you can "borrow" those personality traits and qualities that you desire for yourself. You can begin imagining yourself possessing those same qualities of some self-confident friend or acquaintance. Or, you can "borrow" these traits from some famous person.

"Visualization" through self-hypnosis is of the greatest value in the re-education of the person seeking greater self-esteem. It is just like the most vivid movies, where you project a successful image of yourself on the screen. It sounds so simple that skeptics will reject the concept and the process. Perhaps the problem is that skeptics appreciate things better only after hard efforts. We have been influenced since youth to believe success comes only after long conflicts and struggles. That is the American way of life.

You may be tempted to expect instantaneous results when you begin self-hypnosis for greater self-esteem. If you do not observe expected changes immediately, you may think you are doing it all wrong. You have to be patient.

Perhaps, in the past, you tried other techniques. When there was no overnight miracle, you stopped. Then you ended up back at square one.

First, consciously and deliberately make up your mind that you will work with unrelenting efforts and perseverance. Success will come despite temporary failure, because you are committed to the ultimate goal. Self-hypnosis will work ultimately because you are constantly training your subconscious to react in positive, optimistic, constructive ways. Your program must become as much a part of yourself as possible. Your program must become **you.** You are essentially retraining yourself to respond in an automatic fashion. By self-hypnosis, you literally **must** talk yourself into the feelings you want.

45

One of the earliest examples of this concept was the Biblical exhortation: "As a man thinketh in his heart, so is he." More recently, in the early 1900's Dr. Emile Coue phrased it: "Day by day, in every way, I am getting better and better." Coue's statement is one of the best examples of a self-hypnotic suggestion you must continuously give yourself.

You may assume that a qualified, professional, expensive hypnotherapist can give you more valuable suggestions. In fact, however, they are actually no more valuable than the suggestions you will give yourself. Remember that all hypnosis is really self-hypnosis. For example, if a professional hypnotist clearly suggests "From this time on, you will feel a very high level of self-esteem in all your activities," the subject will subconsciously rephrase it, using the same words, except "I" instead of "You." Thus, the hypnotized person will say subconsciously, "From this time on, I will feel a very high level of self-esteem in all my activities."

What is the simplest, fastest way to learn self-hypnosis? First, become hypnotized and be given a post-hypnotic suggestion that you will be enabled to hypnotize yourself with a specific stimulus. Any good hypnotist, of course, could help you. But, assume you cannot find one. Then, understand and deliberately practice the following methods. You **will** achieve self-hypnosis.

Step-by-Step Method to Self-Hypnosis

Step 1. Relax in your most comfortable chair, sofa, or on your bed.

Step 2. Select a definite spot on the ceiling for eye fixation, that is behind you, so that it will be uncomfortable to keep your eyes there.

Step 3. As you inhale deeply and slowly, repeat aloud or mentally, "sleep." As you exhale, repeat "deep sleep." (Step 4) Continue for a few minutes until you begin to feel drowsy.

Step 5. Suggest to yourself that your eyelids are too heavy to remain open. Your goal is to close your eyes by this technique. As your eyes close of their own choice you reach the first stage of self-hypnosis.

Step 6. Continue to repeat more suggestions like "My eyelids are blinking..." "My eyes are becoming watery..." "My eyelids are becoming too heavy..." "I need to close my eyes..." "As I close my eyes, I will fall into a very deep hypnotic sleep..." "Even though I'll be in a sound hypnotic state, I'll still know where I am and be able to give post-hypnotic suggestions to my subconscious."

Step 7. As your eyelids become heavy and your eyes water, you reinforce these drowsy feelings by continuing positive statements along these same lines. These positive reinforcements help to intensify the state you are in. They facilitate closing your eyes and becoming hypnotized.

Do not feel badly if you do not have immediate results. You merely need to practice more. Late at night, as you begin to fall asleep, is the best time to practice. You are in bed with the lights out and you can practice more easily. At that time, your self-suggestions will

46

drift down into your subconscious as you slip from consciousness to unconsciousness. It is similar to telling yourself to awaken at a specific time. When the suggestion settles into your subconscious, it eventually will actively awaken you in the morning.

Step 8. After you reach eye closure, deepen your hypnotic state by giving yourself these suggestions: "I will fall deeper and deeper into a sound hypnosis as I count to five. By counting to five, I will become more completely relaxed."

Step 9. Continue these suggestions until you feel more at ease. You will assume the state of a thoroughly hypnotized person.

Part of the challenge here is that you do not already know what the hypnotic state feels like. For example, if I say "act angry," you know what being angry feels like. There exists an immediate reference because you have been angry in the past. If you had previously experienced someone hypnotized, you could easily assume those mannerisms you observed.

Some people define the state of hypnotism as being completely relaxed, feeling detached or disassociated, feeling drifting on clouds, or a pleasant, sinking feeling. Others describe it as daydreaming, or as the state just before falling asleep.

Step 10. Since you can direct your responses and feelings continuously, strive to approximate what is described above here.

Step 11. Make the post-hypnotic suggestion that the next time you try to hypnotize yourself you will drift into a sounder, deeper hypnosis when you have relaxed for five minutes and counted to five.

You have surely had the experience of someone telling you it is lunch time and you are hungry, even though it may only be 10 or 11 a.m. In a similar way, you are trying to develop a conditioned response to the count of five that will eventually make your eyes close and put you into hypnosis. Eventually, you will respond instantly to the count of five or any other stimulus you may find to elicit the response. Then, the cues or stimuli become associated with the actions you deserve. With enough practice, merely thinking about the stimulus can cause the response. This kind of ideo-motor behavior occurs when waking as well as in the hypnotic state. Another example of this conditioning is Pavlov's experiments with dogs. They salivated when presented with food while a bell was rung. Eventually, they did the same when only hearing the bell with no food presented. You will achieve the same kind of hypnotic conditioning. Haven't you ever experienced a phone ring when you were expecting a call, even though it did not actually ring? Just as in the visual-imagery technique, during every attempt to attain self-hypnosis, you will try to improve yourself drifting into the hypnotic state. As you deepen the hypnosis, you continue to imagine yourself exactly as you want to be. You actually use the visual-imagery method whether you are hypnotized or not. These pictures focus more clearly as you continually give yourself suggestions.

Step 12. Assume you are relaxing and getting your eyelids to close at the count of five. Then you have passed the first test for hypnosis. Since you have conditioned yourself so far, you are now ready for the next step #12. This second test has been called the "*swallow*" test. Suggest to yourself, as you slowly count to 10, you will develop an irresistible need to swallow one time. Then, you will suggest the need to swallow even before the count of 10. Begin counting. "One... my throat is very dry and I feel a strong need to swallow..." Two... my lips are becoming extremely parched... and I feel an irresistible need to swallow... Three... my throat feels very parched and dried up, so that I cannot keep from swallowing before I count to ten. Four... I feel an uncontrollable need to swallow one time... Five... After I swallow, I will no longer feel a need to swallow. As I swallow, I will fall into a more profound hypnosis." Continue similar affirmations until you actually swallow, which you will do. After you swallow, you will no longer need to suggest swallowing but rather you will suggest you are falling into a deeper and deeper hypnotic state, and that the positive affirmations you **now** will give yourself will always continue to be part of yourself. Here you practice self-imagery, picturing yourself the exact way you want to be. You imagine yourself in a positive, optimistic, achieving, self-confident way.

Step 13. Give yourself suggestions that you will enter the hypnotic realm whenever you relax for five minutes and count to five.

Some beginners state they are too hesitant to give themselves hypnotic self-suggestions, either aloud or only mentally. They forget that they have been doing this same procedure, which I am recommending here, all their lives. It was the same kind of procedure that led you to have your present state of self-confidence initially. Your parents, for example, may have told you directly or indirectly that you were a naughty kid, or worthless in some way. Then, you merely repeated these same false judgments or invalid accusations to yourself mentally. You were not born with a low level of self-esteem. People around you helped talk you into it. And you believed it. Now is the time to begin talking yourself out of it through self-hypnosis. Now is the best time to begin making self-suggestions to yourself. The more you practice this valuable procedure, step-by-step, the more you will develop confidence in giving yourself suggestions. You will not want to hesitate. You will practice enthusiastically.

If you conscientiously follow these instructions, you will have the benefits you want in the quickest possible time. You will witness the positive tangible results of your efforts and self-suggestions.

Deepening Your Self-Hypnosis

There is no absolute rule, of course, but it is usually necessary to pass the first tests of hypnosis before you progress to the others. One exceptional case may occur when you pass the earlier and the later tests, skipping those in between. One common test for the deep state is to give the person a post-hypnotic suggestion: "Your next cigarette will have an especially horrible taste, and you will be unable to take more than three puffs. And, after the third inhalation, you will throw it away."

A good subject will comply with these suggestions in a post-hypnotic state, which is a typical test to determine if you entered into a deeper state of hypnosis. It could happen that someone who has not even completed the eye closure test or any other test may still surprisingly pass the cigarette test.

If you had not experienced the cigarette test, you might have become discouraged. Then, you might not have given yourself therapeutic suggestions because you would feel you had not reached an appropriately beneficial state of hypnosis.

You will want to give yourself whatever helpful suggestions you need, even if you feel nothing has happened. Many people have been temporarily convinced a certain test did not work, but then they were pleased to experience the valuable results of self-hypnosis.

Naturally, as a unique individual, you have your own pattern of needs, values, motives and traits. Even though your symptoms of lower self-esteem may be similar to another person's, you may respond more favorably more quickly as your own special needs are met. This usually occurs on both a conscious and unconscious level.

The best examples of this concept are self-fulfilling prophecies and placebos. If your physician assures you that you are okay and not ill, you will stop worrying and feel better. As a child, when you hurt yourself, your mother's loving kiss and embrace lessened or stopped the pain. A very rational, intellectual, logical approach will not work with the child's pain. Primitive aborigines have been known to die when discovering themselves to be the object of a hated death wish.

The secret to deeper self-hypnosis is the visual-imagery method. You actually picture yourself going deeper and deeper into hypnosis. You see yourself passing the progressive tests. The second secret is to give yourself a posthypnotic suggestion that each attempt will immerse you in a deeper stage as a result of a special stimulus, such as counting to five.

After you have passed the first two basic steps — (1) eye closure and (2) the uncontrollable urge to swallow that is followed by the physical process of swallowing at a specific count, you have achieved the first stage of hypnosis, — the light stage (lethargy). The medium state is the cataleptic stage; the deepest, somnambulistic.

The third test, hand-tingling, will help you determine if you are going deeper.

You have just finished tests 1 and 2. You will be in a completely relaxed state. You will now give yourself these suggestions "As I count off to ten and even before I reach that count of ten, I will feel a light tingling or numb feeling in my left hand." As you deliberately continue to count up to ten, you keep repeating suggestions about the tingling sensations in your left hand. You will continue to practice the methods of visualization described above, remembering the frequent experiences in the past whenever your hand "fell asleep." After you experience an initial feeling of lightness, tingling or numbness, reinforce these sensations by the feedback methods as you did with the eye closure test.

Please remember this important point. Be sure that you give yourself a posthypnotic suggestion that the tingling, light or numb sensation will vanish as you continue to count to 15. You could verbalize, for example, "As I count to 15, the tingling feeling in my left hand will vanish and I will experience only normal feelings. Eleven...the numb feeling is leaving. ... Twelve... Now it is leaving more quickly... Thirteen... I can feel my hand returning to normal ...Fourteen...the tingling has left... Fifteen...my left hand now feels normal.

You can always attempt a variation of this test by saying your nose or left ear will itch by a specific count.

After that test has been achieved, you can proceed to test #4, the foot test. You will recall that the secret to reaching a greater depth of hypnosis consists of visualizing yourself going deeper with each attempt and achieving the next hypnotic test.

For just a reminder, go back to test #3, the hand tingling. After you have succeeded in test #3, use the visualization method to see yourself succeeding with the next test, the foot test. After you have achieved the foot test, #4, you imagine yourself accomplishing #5, the "hand levitation" test. The whole idea is to use each step to enhance a greater openness to the next test. As you add this method on to your posthypnotic suggestions, you will go deeper and deeper into the hypnotic state at a specific stimulus. Then you will activate a conditioned response mechanism that will lower you into progressively more profound levels of hypnosis.

The foot test should be done while lying or sitting down. Imagine your feet stuck to the floor, or your legs too heavy to be raised, until after you reach a definite count. "As I count to five, I will notice very heavy, relaxed, pleasant sensations in both legs. I will feel comfortably relaxed."

Then, count to ten as in previous methods. You can take as much time as you need because there is no time limit. After becoming totally relaxed, use the visualization method to see your legs stuck to the floor. Or, if you are lying down, picture yourself covered by a thick down comforter that is tucked under the mattress so tightly you cannot raise your legs.

If you are sitting up, imagine some "super glue," "krazy glue" or "iron glue" making your feet immobile.

You can use these suggestions for the next part of the test.

"As I deliberately count to ten, it will be impossible to raise my legs. I will try at the count of ten, but it will be completely impossible to raise my legs until I count to 15. At that time, I will be able to raise my legs and the heavy feeling

50

will also leave." You will then proceed with the count as described above and in previous tests, giving yourself the necessary suggestions. After you finish this test, you can use the visualization method to picture yourself succeeding with the hand levitation test #5. Remember, again, to make the post hypnotic suggestion that you will submerge into a deeper state the next time you hypnotize yourself.

Remind yourself, also, to use some of the posthypnotic suggestions listed below about increasing your self-esteem. The whole idea, you will recall, is to use this visualization method to picture yourself as a more self-confident person.

On occasion, you may question why a particular test did not work for you. You may not have conditioned yourself sufficiently, or you were not completely "letting go" enough to enter into a deeper state of hypnosis. Some people need to feel completely in control every step of the way. The situation can be compared to a swimmer deftly entering the water one step at a time. Some people prefer to dive or plunge right in. Others just need to go deeper and deeper until totally under water, even if friends playfully splash at them. Would it be easier to jump in all at once? Perhaps you have had this experience, or have seen it happen.

The analogy will hopefully be clear. The subject seems reluctant to "give up control or let go," when in fact you are even more in control as you submerge into deeper hypnosis.

In reality, hypnotized people who do not raise their legs, actually could do so in an emergency, even without counting to 15. You have entered a state where it is just too much bother to lift your feet. There are two common examples of this state of being. One occurs when you remain in bed in the morning, even though you will be late for work. A second similar experience is when you are high on marijuana — you know where you are and what is happening but you just don't want to be bothered, as you trip out.

The hand levitation test #5 can be attempted after you have succeeded with the previous four. The goal is to have your hand slowly rise to touch your chin. After touching your chin, your hand is slowly lowered to your side as you submerge into a deeper state of hypnosis.

The next time you do the hand-tingling test, strive for a numb sensation in your left hand. After you attain this response, you will give yourself suggestions that your right hand will now rise up to touch your chin.

You can use these suggestions: "As I count up to ten and even before I reach the number ten, I will have an irresistible urge to raise my hand to my chin. As the counting proceeds, my left hand will slowly rise. The urge will become stronger and stronger, and will diminish as soon as I touch my chin. I will then lower my hand and submerge into a very profound state of hypnosis. I will still be more fully aware of what is happening and of my environment. I will be able to give myself helpful posthypnotic suggestions about increasing my self-esteem."

You are striving to feel an involuntary urge to raise your hand. This lifting will be an unconscious movement, completely unlike a deliberate touch, for

51

example, when you are washing your face. If you feel any reluctance for the initial movement, you can begin to do it consciously, but you want the following motions to become automatic.

Finally, when using the preceding suggestions, you do not need to memorize any number of precise words. You will want to understand the concepts and try to integrate them into your actions.

If you feel reluctant to attempt these procedures, try to discover where this hesitance originates. Perhaps ask yourself if you really **do want** to improve your self-esteem. Are you giving yourself enough encouragement? Can you find someone to reward your efforts? Do you really **believe** you can do it? You could act **as if** you believe and **as if** you are succeeding, and then you will.

If you are one of those few skeptics who automatically reject something new out of hand, you may have a different problem that will hinder you from achieving a higher level of self-esteem.

Self-Hypnosis

You can use the following ideas, regardless of how you feel about the self-hypnosis methods and procedures already described. For example, you could use one or both approaches. If you appreciate the previous self-hypnosis methods and if they work for you personally, then use the self-hypnosis statements listed below.

But, if you are unable to use self-hypnosis for any reason, then use the ideas given below as a process of "self-affirmation." Continuously repeat them to yourself, for example, as you shower, bathe, comb your hair or just walk along.

If it helps, copy them on a little card and attach it to your mirror, or place it in your purse, or anywhere you will regularly see it.

If the following statements do not perfectly fit your present needs, then compose your own.

Your short-range goal is to repeat them often enough until you believe them, until they become integrated as a part of your personality.

Your long-range goal is to learn how to act upon them in all phases of your life consistently.

Affirmations for Greater Self-Esteem

There are three stages toward completely believing you will be, can be, and actually are as successful as the next person in business, love, sex, and any other endeavor.

Stage 1: First you have to set your goals. Carefully select goals that are positive, achievable, important, **measurable** and **explicit**.

Use verbs in future tense:

1. I *will* become as self-confident as possible.
2. I *will* become as successful as I possibly can become.

3. I *will* become as effective as others whom I admire.
4. I *will* raise my self-esteem (and self-confidence) to the highest levels.
5. I *will* become a more creative risk-taker in all aspects of my life.
6. I *will* become the person I want to be.
7. I *will* develop more rewarding interpersonal relationships.
8. I *will* learn how to relate better to members of the opposite sex.
9. I *will* take more creative risks today, now, with people I want to become closer to.
10. I *will* strive to live more in the *here* and *now*.
11. I *will* not worry about past mistakes or faults.
12. I *will* not project doubts and fears onto future situations.
13. I *will* make every effort right *here and now* to set some goals.
14. I *will* right *here and now* do what seems best for me and not all possible other people.
15. I *will* not fret over how others judge me.
16. I *will* strive harder to accept responsibility for my own life, decisions and feelings.
17. I *will* give myself credit for all my good qualities, traits and accomplishments.
18. I *will* not be constantly seeking others' approval.
19. I *will* ask for what I need from others.
20. I *will* not deny myself valid, legitimate wants and needs that do not hurt others.
21. I *will* right *here and now* do what's best for me.

Please fill in other relevant goals —

22. I *will* _____

_____

23. I *will* _____

_____

24. I *will* _____

_____

25. I *will* _____

_____

After you have fully memorized the above positive statements, you must affirm them every day. Perhaps you could paste them on your mirror, put them in your top desk drawer **on top**, or in your purse, briefcase, or wherever you will see them. Repeat daily until you feel better.

Stage 2: After you have completed the tasks described above, then begin all over, using the word **can** instead of **will**. "I can become as self-confident as possible."

Stage 3: After you have repeatedly accomplished what is outlined in Stages #1 and #2 above, go on and insert **am** instead of **can** (Stage #2). Then, you will finally be saying "I **am** the person I want to be."

These stages will obviously all take different times for each individual. One person may have to spend 60 days on Stage #1, 30 days for Stage #2, and only 15 days on Stage #3.

The important thing is that you do it for yourself, daily, right here and now.

Chapter 6

Positive Addiction

George "Shotgun" Shuba was originally famous for baseball, but now, thanks to Psychiatrist William Glasser, he will become far more renowned because of his "positive addiction."

In the Summer of 1973, Glasser read a book by Roger Kahn entitled "The Boys of Summer." This book immortalized the Brooklyn Dodgers championship team of 1953. Stars on the team included Jackie Robinson, Roy Campanella, Peewee Reese, Gil Hodges, Duke Snider and many others. Roger Kahn interviewed all the players, including George "Shotgun" Shuba. He discovered something phenomenal that went unnoticed by everyone except Glasser, who used the anecdote to help formulate his own theory about "positive addiction." "Shotgun" Shuba decided to become a major-leaguer at age 16. Instead of going into the Youngstown, Ohio steel millls, he set higher goals. Since he knew he had to become great at hitting major league pitching, George Shuba also knew he had to practice. He wanted a great swing. So George tied a piece of string with a row of knots representing the strike zone from top to bottom. Then, he dangled it from the ceiling in his basement. Everyday from age 16 through his minor and major league careers, George Shuba swung the weighted bat at this strike zone on the string *six hundred times*. That's right. **Six hundred** times.

This incident, reported first by Roger Kahn, became important to William Glasser in developing his theory of "positive addiction."

Positive Addiction is the specific term used by William Glasser, M.D. in his book of the same name (New York: Harper and Row, 1976). His creative concept is that people can become positively addicted, just as alcoholics, heroin addicts, excessive gamblers and others become negatively addicted.

For him, positive addiction is a result of strength, just as negative addiction is an outgrowth of weakness. Positive addiction is a result of efforts toward growth and development. Glasser avers it is possible to become "addicted" to positive ways of behavior that develop the personality as well as the body, for example, jogging, meditating, chanting psalms, listening to classical music and the like, for a definite period every day.

Glasser defines these positive addictions as having nothing to do with drugs, alcohol, or even overeating or drinking too much coffee. Rather, they strengthen people so that they can overcome negative addictions and lead more self-actualizing lives. Although Glasser believes positive addiction tends or appears to come from activities you engage in alone, achieving the positive addiction state (described as a trancelike, transcendental state of mind) it is not absolutely confined to positive addiction. It can occur, in elusive moments, for example, when people are in love. Glasser claims it happened to him while giving a speech to a group.

In these pages, as we continue to explain it a la Glasser, one should keep in mind a particular comparison that he does not make. Humanistic psychologists and those involved in the human potential movement will immediately leap to make comparisons with the "peak experience" phenomenon. From my understanding of both of them, they are somewhat synonymous in the event or in the feeling. But the "peak experience" itself, as defined by Maslow and elucidated by others, is not something that one can train to expect. Positive addiction, however, as described by Glasser, can result from training, as in getting more and more involved in meditating or jogging.

Glasser defines a positive addiction as any activity that person chooses to do following these seven criteria:

1 — any noncompetitive activity, such as jogging;

2 — it usually consumes approximately one hour per day;

3 — you can do it easily without a great deal of mental effort, as in listening to classical music;

4 — you do it alone because it does not depend on others, as in meditating;

5 — you firmly believe in its physical, mental, or spiritual value to yourself;

6 — you subjectively believe that only you measure its improvement value to you;

7 — the activity must be a non-criticizing one so that you can completely accept yourself while you do it.

(Glasser lists six criteria himself, but it seems clearer to make seven so that each concept is a separate one.)

Glasser insists that running:

> perhaps because it is our most basic solitary survival activity, produces the non-self-critical state more effectively than any other practice. If it were up to me to suggest a positive addiction for anyone no matter what his present state of strength, from the weakest addict to the strongest among us, I would suggest running. By starting slowly and carefully, getting checked by a physician if there is any question of health, and working up to the point where one can run an hour without fatigue it is almost certain that the positive addiction state will be achieved on a fairly regular basis. How long this takes depends upon the person, but if there is no attempt at competition and the runner runs alone in a pleasant natural setting, addiction should occur within a year

For the experience to become addicting, you must do it alone to avoid criticism — that is the most crucial point. And that is also why many positive addicts keep quiet about their positive addiction. They have no need to become crusaders. Naturally, it is possible for a jogging fanatic, for example, to try to influence others to adopt his habit, but that is just the result of a different personality need or trait that is outside of the real issue.

The real issue is euphoria. People need to love themselves and have positive feelings of self-worth, and the euphoria of the positive addiction state provides the warm, fuzzy feelings better than any other means.

This is where negative addicts miss the boat. Because they lack feelings of love and self-worth, they seek a substitute feeling through their alcoholism, heroin addiction or gambling addiction. (It is most obvious when a celibate priest takes ice cream or booze to bed instead of a loving woman.)

This chapter cannot possibly, here and now, do justice to Glasser's concept, proofs, and explanations. You may profit from going to his writings on the subject.

While his "Positive Addiction" book is not about directly increasing one's self-esteem, it provides great insights into new ways of looking at how to improve one's self-confidence.

The main point here is that you can use positive addiction to increase your self-confidence. You will want to develop some all-consuming goals, interests and activities. By investing yourself completely in them, you will eventually increase your own feelings of self-confidence. The positive addiction state, you will recall, can only occur if your activities fulfill the seven criteria listed above. Therefore, you will want to try to abide by them in selecting and investing yourself. Writing, for example, may be too much of a self-criticizing function, but writing a daily journal for your personal growth without criticizing the actual words would be productive.

Many people may resist by stating they cannot become joggers because of their health reasons. Any similar excuse could be adduced to avoid involving oneself in any activity. But remember that it need not necessarily be an activity requiring exercise. Perhaps, if you are feeling reluctant right here and now to involve yourself in any all-consuming activity, you might want to ask why you are experiencing some resistance. Then, discuss it with someone close to you or in the extreme event, with a therapist.

Chapter 7

Coping with Rejection

Barbara stepped into the cocktail party after her meeting for just a drink or two. A handsome, well groomed young executive introduced himself to her the moment she arrived. Almost as quickly, they both found out they liked the same classical music, disliked the same movie last week for similar reasons, and had visited the same Club Med. Barbara began feeling the sudden joy of a possible new friendship, when her new man left her for a refill on both their drinks. But her wine, her hopes, and the bright young man who carried them never returned. Barbara slyly pretended not to notice as he became more involved in conversation with an extremely beautiful blonde. Her pain increased as she noticed them leaving together.

Habitually, Barbara began her comparison checklist. The blonde was prettier, thinner, younger, and probably brighter than she. Sulking her way through animated guests, she went home feeling angry at herself, getting more and more depressed. Vowing never to be so foolish in the future, she would no longer hope for friendship or love with just a few moments of talk.

Barbara had been rejected. She reacted as do most people in a similar situation, making a firm resolution to avoid any similar occurrence. Such resolutions, however, offer no real insurance nor protection against rejection, as inevitable a force in our lives as solar/nuclear energy. Barbara needed to learn if you aren't rejecting or being rejected, you aren't really living. Rejection is a *Guaran-God-Damn-Teed* part of life. You just can't avoid it. That is the point where you begin the downward spiral to a lower level of self esteem, or at least, not be enabled to hold your own. Or not make the progress towards greater self esteem that you want.

You have to learn how to detect that point where you may lose your equilibrium. Then pull yourself up short. In Barbara's case she could have done a number of effective things. She could have reminded herself that rejection is an inevitable fact of life and then begin a new search. Or she could have avoided making erroneous comparisons with the blonde. How could Barbara prove for example, the blonde was really smarter? Barbara had learned the bad habit of making faulty comparisons, and then giving the benefit of the doubt to the blonde instead of to herself.

Unless you do want to become a hermit, it is helpful to learn more about the heartbreaking phenomenon of rejection, how you presently attempt to cope and what all this means for increasing your self-esteem.

Do You Expect Rejection?

If you seem to experience rejection more than others, it may be because your behavior invites it. Michelle, a lovely girl in her early twenties, continually gripes about the way men relate to her. "I try everything to make my lovers relaxed. But they always seem to leave me...I was just recently enchanted by a perfect guy. Whenever he called I did my best to be pleasing. All went well for months. Then subtle signs appeared. He became late for dates. Then he cancelled. Finally, he did not even show up. I was so hurt I really like him and did not want to be demanding. But the more giving I seemed to be, the worse he seemed to treat me. He didn't even call me for two weeks. When I got to see him, I cried too much. He vowed there was no one else, he liked me very much, and that I was too good for him. **Now**, I agree, of course. But at the time I didn't want to hear him say that. I became too graspingly dependent, and he became more indifferent."

"One awful August weekend was the end. He'd invited me sailing on Lake Michigan. When I called to ask where we would meet, he wasn't home. All Friday and Saturday I kept phoning. First, a busy signal then no answer. Well, you might guess Sunday morning was a nightmare. I was angry and anxious. I taxied over to his condo.

"Just as the cab pulled around the corner, he was leaving with a stunning redhead. I knew they had just spent the night together. I hoped to become invisible. He spied me and came over. "You **told** me there was no one else," I sobbed hysterically. "He vowed again it was true and he just met her last evening at a party."

"At home, I fell apart again. The tragedy is all my affairs end the same way, just as painfully."

Michelle had fallen into a pattern. Psychologists have long known about rejection-prone personalities. People with low self esteem tend to view themselves as losers. They ask for rejection because of their overly meek demeanor. They almost seem to be saying by their behavior, "See how sweet and nice I am and how rotten you are." When the other person begins to behave in the projected role, almost like a self-fulfilling prophecy, the first person can always feel justified: "I told you so."

Just as the overly dependent/compliant personality invites rejection by a "Hurry, step-on-me" demeanor, so also can the overly aggressive individual. By assaulting others, these people hope to protect themselves. It's almost as if they want to risk rejection by hostility rather than by being too agreeable. Their manners are poor. They appear offensive to all types. They want to avoid closeness by warding others off. Margaret always provoked rejection as an excuse for not having to test her own inability to become emotionally intimate. Subconsciously, she courted rejection by projecting an overly aggressive personality.

60

Your self-concept can lead you to do one of the above like either Michelle or Margaret. Neither had a normal level of self-esteem, nor knew how to raise theirs.

Overeager Fantasies Can Lead to Rejection

Linda launched relationships doomed to failure. She like most of us had an ideal mate pictured in her fantasies. Also like many of us, she created the false front she believed would attract that uniquely super man. You can **initially** attract someone with a facade, but eventually that person will see thru it. And desiring what you initially seemed to be, upon discovering reality your partner is sorely disappointed. At that point, you may redouble your efforts to make the facade all the more desirable. You can quickly learn to become too much like the wrong person, rejecting your authentic self.

You can only develop true emotional intimacy by being your own congruent self. You have to develop a valid level of self-esteem founded on truth and reality, not on an unrealistic expectation of someone you can never become, nor would even really want to be.

There is a valid distinction here between a phoney facade and a realistic expectation of growth. You should expect success, and become the person you want to be.

The process of Idealization can operate in reverse for you when your over-active imagination makes a splendid hero/heroine out of an ordinary person. Your strong desire to discover that special someone distorts your perception. You see your intended as endowed with outstanding qualities, and you shower him/her with seemingly unlimited affection.

As reality becomes more apparent, you may put the person down for not being what you want your mate to be. Nor could your partner want to be that way. You realize: "Hey, I'm getting all this hostility and I'm just being myself."

Your initial lack of self awareness has lead to faulty perceptions. The experience is painful. That can lead to even greater fears of rejection or unwillingness to take risks.

How Rejection Can Inhibit You

Your desire to prevent pain of rejection causes you to constrain your life, avoiding adventures that could bring happiness. Being rebuffed then leads you to increase your self-protection. This happened to Audrey. "I'm really a shy person. After sometime alone in the big city, I decided I needed to take a little risk. One sunny afternoon on Oak Street beach, a friendly man introduced himself. We had an enjoyable chat, and exchanged phone numbers. A few weeks later I had an extra ticket to the symphony. It was almost impossible for me to call, but he was free. He looked as great in a business suit as he had in swimming trunks.

"The date was fun. But he never called back. I'm **never** going to take the initiative again."

Feelings of rejection in any business or social encounter can be as devastating as any emotional putdown. Bill can be rejected for a job interview

61

or Marcy could feel rejected at a party. It usually happens because people with low self-esteem are overly sensitive. People who are intensely egotistic can be extremely vulnerable. They fear rejection precisely because they need to protect their own feelings of grandiose importance. By putting themselves at the heart of the universe, they are unable and unwilling to respect other's feelings. By responding hostilely to rejection, they seem to be saying: "How could you not pay attention to me. Don't you appreciate who I am?" Such pompous grandiose behavior can exist not only in those who seem strong and overly assertive, but also in those who appear shy and withdrawing.

Ask yourself if your pain and anger at rejection is a mask for your low self-esteem and feelings of false, exaggerated self-importance. The person who apparently rejected you may merely have had other plans. If you feel personally put down, you may have an overly strong need to control or manipulate others. Yet **you** do not want to be controlled. So, why should others acquiesce to your ideas when it is not helpful to them?

Fears of rejection, then, can be caused by unconscious egotism or needs to control others. Another cause is even more devious.

Fear of Rejection Can Conceal Fear of Success

You would be amazed how many people fear success. The reason is clear. When you achieve success you are supposed to be an adult, independent, in charge of your life.

Consider Mimi, an attractive professional who could have unlimited single lovers, but prefers married men. "I agree my probabilities of building a lasting relationship with any of my lovers are really slim. But if I don't win, I won't have to blame myself or my own weaknesses. After all, men **almost always** go back to their wives. There is so much more to risk with a single man. He might jilt me because he no longer says he appreciates my companionship. I never have that risk with married men." Mimi is an example of how a significantly low level of self-esteem leads one to fear success.

Ann had another method to avoid success. She was an intelligent, beautiful, well-educated, thirty-one year old woman who had affairs with many desirable men. They all ended quickly, because she rejected her lovers first for the slightest reasons. Recently, she dated a wealthy broker who really needed her and longed for intimacy. She paled at the prospect that he might reject her first. So, she ended it.

Ann's pattern was clear. If she rebuffed him first, she exults in the power, and also reduces risks of pain. She does not see the hollow victory. Ann can never grow without taking risks. Everyone basically wants growth, but finds it hard to risk the changes.

People develop a broad range of defenses to avoid risks. One of the most self-defeating is the next one.

Are You Attracted to Those Who Reject You?

The following dynamics seem clearer in the lives of women. Although most women and men invest a great amount of energy avoiding rejection, many women are attracted only to the man whose behavior says: "I'm uninterested in you."

It usually traces back to her childhood, where her father was **the** man. But naturally, she could never be **the** woman in his life. Later as an adult, the lover rebuffing her overtures is viewed as daddy. Hooked on her first infatuation with Dad, she can only relive it by feeling rejected. She has not outgrown this stage or worked through it correctly. She always seems to be falling into the same trap with a man who casts her aside, as she struggles to recreate her first attraction.

Recently, a woman client came to SECS to discuss her lover. Sara's parents were divorced in her childhood and she felt spurned by her father. Her recent rejection by her stockbroker lover stirred up again all her old pain from age nine. Even her gestures and voice were those of a child as she pouted. Sara could not even get angry at him because that would mean, unknown to her, also getting angry at her father. She would then have lost him forever.

Psychologists increasingly point out patients who have remained together in mutual rejection, each personality venting its own passive aggression against the other. One partner may break the pattern and actually begin to pursue: "Here I am. I'm yours. I'm not rejecting you anymore." Then the pursuer may back down, too, and become the pursued person. Then, he or she begins to threaten the other with rejection. Basically, each partner is using the rebuffs to re-create childhood competition for that parent of the opposite sex.

To mollify past ghosts, a person may pursue rejection in myriads of ways. Suppose, for example, Sara as a young girl competed with her mother for her dad's love. She feels hurt everytime her parents go into the bedroom together, leaving her alone in her own bed. Despite her suffering over this rejection, her pain would be even **greater** and **deeper**, if she had "ever" really won her old man, because then she would risk losing her mother's love. Later, in adulthood, Sara or any other woman may duplicate this pattern. Her security comes from being spurned. She cannot seem to recognize all men are not her old man, and that she is no longer a child.

Not all rejections, however, are self-induced. Some just happen.

When Bad Luck Happens

The hurt can seem infinite when one person just dumps another.

Stan was an absolute genius in his ability to manipulate a woman's fear of rejection. On the first date he was always coming on strong. But on the second date his aloofness would raise her anxiety. She can't figure out what she could have done wrong. Then, as she is on the brink of total insecurity by the third date, he seduces her sexually. Then, he never calls her again. Her self-esteem is ruined. (He was always impotent and afraid to go on for fear she would find out. But, of course she never knew this.) After continuing in this pattern for years, Stan finally came to SECS for sex therapy. It did help him, but not all the women he had previously rejected in his mistaken quest for the Wonder Woman who could cure him.

These women all blamed Stan for hurting them. Few people ever realize no one else hurts you. You hurt yourself. You experience the pain of rejection only when **you** have first rejected part of yourself. It is an illusion to imagine the feeling was put there by the rejecting lover. Whenever a man stands up a woman, he merely chose to do something else, however rude and thoughtless his decision and behavior may be. But the suffering she experiences is caused by her own feelings of low self-esteem, which she does not understand. She falsely assumes a wrong reason for the rejection, such as she is old and ugly. If she could begin to accept all of herself and increase her self-esteem, she would not mull over all her doubts and fears. Her increasing self-esteem would literally lift her out of the miasma.

Self-esteem is the only guard against rejection.

How Rejection Lowers Self-Esteem

Whether rejection just happens, or you actively seek it out, your self-concept will surely suffer, unless it is very strong. Even people with strong, validly high levels of self-esteem do not enjoy being rejected. Joan was an intelligent, sophisticated funeral director who met an exciting man at a party. He was married. After an adventurous affair, he actually even got a divorce. "He remarried quickly — but not to me. I was furious. I may not have married him, but did want to be asked. My outrage made me jump too quickly into another bad affair — but that is a different story." Joan's self-esteem was surely deply afflicted. Her self-esteem was always too dependent on others' estimation. The more conforming you become, the more vulnerable you will be to rejection. You must learn to develop your own integrity, and not ever again let your self-esteem depend on others. You cannot be wounded by rejection or rendered impotent by fear of it. Millions of men become impotent because of this same fear of rejection or failure. (See Dauw, *Stranger in Your Bed, A Guide to Emotional Intimacy*. Nelson-Hall, Chicago, 1979).

Let Your Fears Help You Grow

Pain need not be always negative. It can be viewed as a warning. Remember that anyone who loves or seeks love must risk rejection. Because you don't want your loved ones to reject you, you become overly cautious in dealing with them. You forget that you have to earn love. It is not handed you on a silver platter. So you need to learn how to become more understanding and accepting of others. Fear of rejection, then, can have positive aspects as long as you do not let yourself become paralyzed by it.

Count on Your Self-Esteem

You cannot remold yourself to fit another person. You have to increase your own self-esteem so that you can grow more quickly to become the person you want to be. In fact, one of the biggest mistakes you could make would be to try to make yourself over to please another person. Do not reject yourself first. Remember that rejection is only one feeling, and you can become bigger than **any one** emotion. Naturally, if you seem to be experiencing too many rejections, you should take a serious look in the mirror of psychotherapy or sex therapy. At the very least, you may be making seriously wrong decisions, such as choosing the wrong partners or the wrong jobs. (See Dauw, *Up Your Career, 3/E*, Waveland Press: Prospect Heights, Illinois, 1980.)

You need to discover your own true feelings. Otherwise, your self-esteem diminishes every time someone walks over you or spurns you. By finding your true feelings and your own self, you can begin to make intimate emotional contact with others. You do not need beauty or riches to find someone with whom you can make true contact or discover deep intimacy. Everyone has the ability to grow her own authentic self or become truly real.

When someone rejects you, he or she is not necessarily saying you are bad; merely that you are not right for them at this moment. You may be too high powered for him and he is looking for a fawning, dependent doe. You may be a dynamite career woman and he is seeking a motherly cook. The French say: "To understand all is to forgive all." Psychologists paraphrase it "To understand all is to learn better to forgive yourself."

Just as we have Alcoholics Anonymous and Gamblers Anonymous, we need to develop a "Feedback Anonymous." You should never let someone just hang there, twisting slowly in the wind. You could take a considerate initiative toward assisting everyone's self-esteem by volunteering: "I no longer want to see you at this time because _____." Then fill in your own true feelings, that may help the other person understand. You could express the truth. It is better to help the other partner understand rather than be left hanging.

Regardless of what may be the pain, you can learn to keep it under control. You need to resist the temptation to hate or reject yourself. Remember, whatever the pain and suffering you are not alone. Everyone else feels rejection too. Most people managed to make it. You can use it to learn better how to increase your self-esteem. If all else seems to fail, try this method of **first aid for rejection.**

First Aid for Rejection

The secret is to face your feelings immediately, own them, and literally **confront** them. Do not try to escape or bottle up your pain in little suppression/repression pills.

You will be able to get over these feelings of being spurned or hurt once you fully experience them.

Consider these helpful exercises in a step-by-step plan.

First, replay in your mind exactly what happened, just like instant replay on T.V. Use your imagination. Recreate the event in detail and try to become more fully aware of how you feel. Call forth again all the bad feelings.

Second, replay this event as explained above several times. Repeating this scene will diminish its intensity, even if it occurs only in your imagination. You may only need to do this a few times or you may have to do it 20 or 25 times. That number depends on how much you hurt.

Third, exaggerate the event. Try to fantasize what would have happened if you carried the whole scene and all its feelings to an exaggerated ending. Suppose for example, you are a woman who has just been spurned. Take time to imagine it as in step one and step two above. Then, picture him also saying you are ignorant, repulsive and smell so bad you'll never get another date forever. If you give yourself this permission to call forth all the remote possibilities, then the actual occurrence will lose its pain.

These three steps are necessary to bring the fiasco out into the open, into your awareness, so you can be certain to experience it. Then you can extinguish them rather than have them cause a deep emotional cancer. You need to confront them immediately.

You can use the same technique if you suffer from **fear** of rejection or even fear of failure, whether in your sex life or career life. You can project your fear into the future as a kind of vaccination or psychological immunization.

Suppose you have to call someone for a date or a party or because you have a theatre ticket. You fear your friend will reject you. Assume this fear is keeping you from calling. Fantasize the conversation you may expect in a negative fashion. Imagine a resounding "No!". Do not imagine a "maybe" or "yes". Remember the purpose of this exercise is to extinguish your negative feelings — your fear of rejection. You can do this extinguishing by first evoking the image of being spurned.

Then, continue to expand on that thought and engage in even more related probabilities. You will call forth negative feelings the event could cause.

Third, expand the possible negative rejection and accompanying emotions. Imagine your friend will not go and would not even bother to spit on you. Suppose your friend even suggests you'd be no fun ever, even in bed. Fantasize the worst. If you follow these instructions, they will **not** reduce your self-esteem slowly. These methods will bring your fears out into the open awareness now, consciously and by choice at this particular time, here and now. Then, you will avoid having them hinder you for the rest of your life.

The exposed and confronted fear will evaporate. You will be enabled to go about the process of continuing to increase your self-esteem.

Chapter 8

Managing Your Moods

Jane was describing to her therapist how her moods were ruining her relationship with Peter. "He's a neat guy. Our relationship is the best one I've ever had. I hate to ruin it. But I'm so moody. It bugs him. And I hate myself for it."

Jane's moodiness was also severely hurting her own self-esteem but she did not even realize it at the time. To increase your self-esteem, you really need to understand what your moods are, how they make you feel and what you can do about it.

A mood can be a strange thing. Everyone seems to understand when we say "My wife's in a good mood" or "my husband is in a bad mood."

Usually, what most people mean, however, is unclear. To state you are "in a mood" is like saying we do not know exactly why you are behaving the way you are at this moment here and now. Although you can describe your behavior, we cannot pinpoint what determines it. You may be suggesting that certain boundaries are influencing your actions, and that any efforts by you or others to modify those boundaries will be more successful at some times rather than others. Our moods are barometers measuring our world.

To alter your moods, first you need to understand the differences between temperament (basic personality traits, emotions), and mood.

Temperament is a lifelong tendency toward certain moods. Thus, we say people are naturally serious or very enthusiastic. An emotion is a strong feeling that may occur more frequently in one mood than in another. For example, a strong feeling of elation may occur when making love unexpectedly at 3 p.m., while you were in a good mood all day anyway. On the other hand, too little sleep may put you in a bad mood so that you more easily experience deeper feelings of anger or hostility. These emotions may depend on your underlying mood.

You can still be both happy or sad in the same mood. James Thurber was quoted about his times in the theatre when he "laughed and cried at the same time." A clear example could be in *My Fair Lady* when Eliza Doolittle was first enabled to speak "The Rain in Spain." We are very pleased about her relief in accomplishing it all, and cry because the scene was handled so beautifully. Similarly, you probably can remember being both loving and urgent in the same mood or like small children both tired and hyperactive.

Your mood may make you temporarily ready for definite feelings or emotional reactions. Whenever you label someone "moody," you are observing more apparent behavior changes more frequently and more deeply than most people experience them.

What causes moods? Three basic factors can cause a mood in you. Organic factors are primary: drugs, glands, biochemistry, nutrition, and other bodily changes. Environmental factors are a second cause that are clear to see or hear, such as loud rock music or disco beat.

A third factor may be episodic influences: successes, failures, interruptions, frustrations, surprises, and the like.

Mood Temperature Checklist

Each statement below describes some moods. Go through the list four times each day for one week. List words that clarify your feelings. Your first statement is always best; so write quickly. After a week, a pattern should stand out. If you experience yourself in a particular mood at a time of day, try to associate what is happening with your emotions. You can find ways to bring about more better moods and fewer bad ones.

Active	Overjoyed	Elated	Jittery	Energetic
Passive	Meditative	Thoughtful	Satisfied	Regretful
Doubtful	Sleepy	Cynical	Humorous	Other-Centered
Fearful	Uptight	Considerate	Egotistic	Self-Centered
Proud	Angry	Vigorous	Strong	Warm-Spirited
Sad	Loving	Exhausted	Weak	Eager
?_____	?_____	?_____	?_____	?_____

These episodic factors are more susceptible to work on self-esteem. You can arrange to reduce failures, for example, and increase successes. As your successes mount, so also will your greater feelings of self-esteem. Then you will be enabled to control your moods.

You need to raise your self-esteem to have more successes, and the better, warm, positive feelings that follow. Then your moods will change for the better. On the other hand, each time you are better enabled to manage your moods, you will also feel much better about yourself, which increases self-esteem. Finally, you can begin to see how one process aids and reinforces the other: you manage your moods for more positive feelings and greater self-esteem; also, you predict success, work hard for it, feel better and can manage your moods more effectively.

	9 AM	12 Noon	5 PM	9 PM

Monday

Tuesday

Wenesday

Thursday

Friday

Saturday

Sunday

Specialists seem to disagree about the other factors that contribute to your moods. Researchers who are biologically oriented believe moods are almost totally regulated by your nutrition and body chemicals. The two that receive most study are serotonin and norepinephrine, which are both present at various receptor sites in the brain and highly concentrated in places associated with drives such as sex, hunger and thirst. If you have too much of one or more of these amines, your moods can range from pleasant elation to intense anxiety and ultimately hypomania or hypermania. When you have too little, you may become depressed, or even suicidal. Some investigators theorize the level of chemicals such as salt in the blood — your electrolyte balance — may influence your mood control.

Some researchers suggest that for the average person, mild forms of mood swings have few if any biological factors. Gynecologists state one exception may be women around their menstrual period. Some may experience more depression and irritability. Most psychologists disagree with those statements and prefer to attribute it to learned behavior. They assert most women can learn to modify their own behavior or control it at that time of the month.

The mild mood swings we all have are mostly a reaction to daily events, which is where the mood barometer gauge here can be helpful. You will want to record your feelings at certain times of the day as indicated to discover your moods more clearly. Then, you will be in a much better position to change the preceding circumstances that may cause them.

Society's present attitudes towards moods seems more enlightened. In older days, bad moods were things to be forgotten or avoided. Presently, however, people are becoming more willing to examine them and use them as springboards for growth. That is the main point of this chapter, that you can learn from your moods and change them for your personal growth and development, especially the increase of your self-esteem.

Mind-altering drugs such as marijuana and cocaine are becoming more prevalent. More people are experimenting with altering their states of consciousness. Some younger people seem less tolerant of bad moods and want to alter them with alcohol, pills or other drugs.

This lack of tolerance for discomfort extends to work. Today, if a worker wakes up in a bad mood, she/he is less likely to go to work. Previously, more employees were more willing to go to their jobs even if they had a headache, a virus, or minor flu.

A bad mood means you are pessimistic about the future. It is an all-encompassing depressed feeling that tends to creep in as a physical sluggishness and desire to do nothing. You feel unable to function very well. Instead of throwing themselves into a cause or movement, people are more likely to fight these moods with overeating or drinking or succumbing to T.V.

One major problem you have when attempting to alter moods with drugs or alcohol is that you cannot predict what will happen. Few people will just experience, for example, a cocaine high. They want to drink too heavily at the same time or even smoke pot at the same time.

Janie asserted she had to smoke a joint every day in the morning before leaving for work, so that she could tolerate her boring secretarial duties. Then, in the evening, she liked to inhale coke and slowly smoke pot. Janie claimed the exhilaration of the coke cut down the lethargic mood caused by the grass. Then, she believed she felt twice as mellow and not sluggish.

Janie's measured self-esteem was low. She needed to realize it was easier, cheaper and better for her to control her moods by methods described in this book rather than by drugs.

With alcohol, you may experience an increase in talkativeness and a decrease in shyness, after small doses. For most people, however, alcohol merely reinforces your dominant mood. Aggressive people who drink too much may merely become more hostile.

Young male subjects in one study in a small group setting who used amphetamines became more talkative, more self-centered and more confident. When antihistamines, usually prescribed for allergies, were given in a laboratory experiment, the participants became sluggish and withdrawn and less socially cooperative. Thus, if you have to be in a sharp mood in a leadership situation, you should be careful about antihistamines and never mix them with alcohol.

Drugs and alcohol, then, do not really change bad moods into good ones. You need to apply the methods of this chapter and also the whole book, as suggested earlier.

Here are some more specific and practical methods. Consider the Mood Temperature Checklist in this chapter. If possible, add in some more adjectives that seem to describe you more clearly. Ask yourself questions like the following: "How do I really feel here and now?" "What may have caused this emotion?" "Have I felt like this previously?" "What caused it then?" "What would I change?" "How could I change that feeling?"

Try to identify your pattern of moods. If it's a pleasant mood, you will especially want to identify those factors so that you can repeat them. Then, when you discover what stimuli or causes lead to bad moods, you will want to change them.

The easiest way to change depends upon major factors in your personality, such as your interests. What do you really like to do? What turns you on? If you enjoy movies, or swimming, you may try to do that. But, remember, if you are in a bad mood, make sure you go to a comedy rather than some movie that will merely make your bad mood worse.

Folk wisdom suggests many prescriptions for first aid. Among them are exercise, relaxation techniques, all types of commercial entertainment. Do something good for somebody which will really cheer you up. Start with yourself. Learn to give yourself more honest pleasure rather than punish yourself. Bake a cake. Enjoy a long conversation with a friend. Deliberately buy an item you may not need. Duck away from harsh reality for a few moments with the right book or magazine. Since a bad mood is oppressive, get out from under it with small pleasures that can reduce your pressures.

71

How can you get a girlfriend, boyfriend or boss out of a bad mood? Remember that your mood is the barometer of your ego state. You will want to aid your friend to change her ego state. Offer respect, and warm, honest caring. Give her sincere compliments and other warm fuzzies. Try to support her ego.

But watch out for the trap. Some people will try to manipulate you. If someone learns that you respond to her bad mood with more tender, loving care, she may tend to exploit you. Or, if he becomes too selfish when in a good mood, he may become too much of a problem in other ways.

If someone always seems to be putting you in a bad mood, ask yourself if she/he is deflating your ego accidentally or on purpose to satisfy his or her own neurotic needs. You need to investigate whether a person with low self-esteem is controlling your moods.

Because moods are all a part of life, we should not be afraid of them. If the methods in this chapter and book do not seem to be helping you as well or as quickly as you want, then you will want to call a good psychologist for professional help.

Remember, a mood by definition is something that will pass. Like the weather, if you don't like it, cheer up. It won't be the same for too long.

For they can conquer who believe they can.
—Virgil

Chapter 9

Self-Esteem and Humor

Skipping down a hospital corridor one day, a clown, whose funny face is familiar to most Americans, spied a tiny girl with a doll of his likeness propped up in bed beside her. The girl shouted out his name, causing the astounded nurse who had been feeding the patient to run for the doctor. The girl, suffering from the withdrawn, silent state of catatonic schizophrenia, had been speechless for eight months. The clown continued the communication, and after that breakthrough her condition improved.

"Laughter is the best medicine" has been an age-old theory. Psychologists have long theorized that negative emotions cause negative chemical changes in the body. Recently, it has been suggested that even such diseases as cancer may be produced, or at least fostered, in some cases by harmful stress. If this is true, could the reverse also be possible? Could positive feelings be associated with or even cause positive chemical changes leading to greater well-being?

Could a person be cured by laughter? Norman Cousins, former editor of Saturday Review, became convinced that humor has a curative effect. Doctors reported it in the conservative New England Journal of Medicine (12/23/76).

Cousins's malaise apparently began in 1964 when he returned from Russia, physically and emotionally exhausted. Physical aches and pains deepened into a kind of arthritic paralysis.

Connecting tissues in Cousins's spine began disintegrating. Physicians predicted only one chance in 500 of recovery. Cousins believed the maxim "Most people never discover until it is too late that life is a "Do-It-Yourself" project." So he became actively involved in his own recovery, much more so than most typical patients with most usual diseases. He remembered reading that "adrenal exhaustion" often contributing to arthritic and similar diseases had been caused by negative feelings. The alert patient believed such positive emotions as hope, love, a stong willingness to live, laughter and joy may be the best therapy or at least have curative effects.

As one part of a complete program, Cousins decided to change his attitudes, to reduce his anxiety by working on his self-esteem. He may not have been thinking precisely in the same terms as this chapter and book, but he provides an interesting example of how laughter cures, how laughter/humor can increase your self-esteem.

Cousins checked out of an impersonal hospital into a hotel. The challenge was to find laughter while stretched out on his back in pain; he decided to make himself laugh. Allen Funt of "Candid Camera" fame sent classics of his best films. Cousins discovered a few minutes of belly laughter had a pain-deadening effect, just like anesthesia, that earned him a few hours sleep. Whenever pain awakened him, he turned on the films and laughter again. Cousins continuously read humor books.

Almost to his disbelief, after eight hours of therapy, Cousins moved his thumbs with less pain. As time went on, doctors found the connective tissues in joints and spine improving. Believing in success and making positive self-fulfilling prophecies, Cousins continued to make progress daily. He could return to work, although freedom from all pain was 10 years away. Best of all, he knew he was avoiding death, predicting cures and expecting health.

In the two examples above, the failings of modern medicine were being conquered by treating the person's spirits, mind, or soul. Witch doctors have understood this for centuries in Africa. Dr. Albert Schweitzer worked closely with the witch doctors, both making referrals to them and accepting referrals from them. All this suggests strong placebo effects on bodily improvements from the use of humor and laughter.

In his recently published book, *Laugh After Laugh — The Healing Power of Humor*, Raymond A. Moody, Jr., M.D., suggests the term "breaking up," as we often describe paroxysms of laughter, as becoming literally true. Continued laughter makes your muscles go limp. You may not hold a glass tightly and drop it. Tension or a surplus of energy is released by laughing. Somehow, these positive emotions have therapeutic effects.

Moody concludes there is an important place in medicine for laughter, regardless of how it works on the body. He wants modern medicine to bring forth this ancient idea again. Psychologists and doctors have been taught to discover everything about patients — age, appetite, sleeping habits, sexual behavior, physical activities and the like. But they were not specifically taught to inquire about one's sense of humor.

Moody believes your appreciation of jokes and ability to laugh is just as valid an indicator or predictor of your health as anything else.

Doctor Moody believes humor should be introduced into the lives of the sick and disabled. Psychologists have always tried to do the same with the depressed. Moody wants to convince you there is a clear connection between your sense of humor and your will to live. These relationships have much to do with humor's anesthetic effect on pain, as in Norman Cousins's situation.

Psychologists suggest humor distracts your attention from pain. Clearly, some types of pain, like migraine headaches, are intensified by muscle tensions that you may unknowingly increase. When you laugh, you relax muscles, reduce tensions, alleviate stresses, and eventually increase your self-esteem.

Surely, the physical effects of your laughter are obvious. It has been a mystery for centuries how all this aids you. Little research exists. Awareness of laughter's magic led the medieval surgeon, Henri de Mondeville, to keep his patients' spirits up by telling jokes. Kings had court jesters. Queen Elizabeth I had Richard Tarlton to "cure her melancholy better than all her physicians."

How can you become more humorous? Witty? Full of Fun? You can develop a personal growth program to use humor to increase your self-esteem. Perhaps you can find even better ways than those suggested by Moody.

1. Think up more practical jokes. Develop more "Laugh-In" days. You can make an April Fool's Day or Halloween costume day occur more often. Those who know you may not accept it 365 days per year. But you can deliberately set aside more time to create more humor. A harmless old prank may become more curative than humorous.

2. Enjoy humorous movies or TV specials by your favorite comedians instead of dreary dramas.

3. Attend a comedy club instead of just a bar or nightclub.

4. Ask your librarian, bookstore or neighbor for jokes/humorous books.

5. Develop your own humor-fun places. Moody recommends "humor environments." He wants to set up rooms with "fun machines," piping in laugh-sound effects, jokes, cartoons and the like, with costumes and masks for you to dress in.

6. Learn how to cultivate a sense of humor that seems natural to you. You have heard many friends say: "I can't remember jokes." Fact is, they have not yet made a decision to try, to learn, to use that part of their memory. Actually, jokes are easier to learn than most everything else you already learned, like math or languages. (By now, you should be becoming more aware of the value of doing all these suggestions.)

7. Commit yourself to developing a humorous outlook on life. Take yourself less seriously. Try to laugh at events that cause stress to others. Your humor will help stop self-defeating behaviors.

You will laugh rather than cry at daily frustrations. Perhaps you could begin slowly and easily by learning one good joke. Practice by telling three people that day, as an aid to help you remember it. Associate it with common things. Dan, for example, has two favorite beer jokes that he relates when he sees someone swigging a beer.

Humor will increase your feelings of self-esteem, in general, because you will live a happier life. Laughter will help you build self-confidence at any given moment, in particular, because your unique joke will make people smile with you and give you positive feedback at that one moment when you tell that funny story. Each small reward in its own fashion reinforces your overall feelings of well-being.

Humor is not the magic panacea that cures all diseases. Even though it has worked for some does not mean it will instantly help you. And you should not blame someone who does not seem to be helped.

But your perseverance will pay off over time. If you expect a positive result, you will experience one. Plan to let your humor make you feel better. Laughter will then increase your self-esteem.

Be always displeased with what thou art, if thou desirest to attain to what thou art not; for where thou hast pleased thyself, there thou abidest. But if thou sayest I have enough, thou perishest. Always add, always walk, always proceed. Neither stand still, nor go back nor deviate.

—Augustine

Chapter 10

Jealousy...and Self-Esteem

"Be honest." That oft-repeated admonition may not always be quite the thing to do, at least as far as jealousy and your self-esteem is concerned.

Take, for example, your past sex life. Should you ever confess all to your new friend, lover or partner? Some people, of course, can't resist talking about their "conquests" because it inflates their ego (not their real self-esteem). Many men think discussing their past love (or sex) lives will make them appear more "macho" to their new lovers.

But take a leaf from the book of life that women own, my friends. Women seldom, if ever, talk about their past affairs, and if they do, it is usually only after much prompting. Even then, they may only talk so that they can re-assure their new lover that they like him better than their old lover or lovers.

Betty and Allen might be a good illustration. They were married in their middle twenties. Neither had been married before, and they had lived together for three months as a sort of "trial period." Allen had been around quite a bit, much more so, Betty thought, than she had.

For some time prior to their marriage and for almost a year afterwards Allen hinted around that since he had confessed (read that as "bragged" about) his past love life, she should as well.

Betty had been warned by several friends to tell only what she had to, but when Allen confessed a rather embarrassing moment of his, Betty decided to tell him of her own sexual past. The trouble was, Allen wasn't ready for it.

In retrospect, Betty realized that Allen was really hoping she would "confess" to virtual celibacy before she met him. Although he knew she was not a virgin when they met, Allen still had an idea that *his* wife was not promiscuous, not "easy" and definitely not used.

But at that time, Betty thought she was being honest. (She was soon to learn that you can only do that with a partner who has a high level of self-esteem). Betty revealed how she had lost her virginity to a high school track star and Allen said he understood because he had been a jock, too, and knew how attractive they were to some girls. But then he pressed for details and innocently enough, thinking her husband was liberated, Betty told him several amusing stories of trying to make out in cars, of being caught per-forming fellatio by her roommate, and several other adventures.

Allen pressed for still more details, masochistically, as Betty later realized. She spoke of several other casual affairs, then of a torrid affair with her college music teacher. She had fallen in love with him, she said, but knew it was hopeless, because he was married. She told of two years of hopeless love, of letting herself be used. Then she talked of getting over it with a series of other men, and finally, meeting Allen.

Betty thought she had a man whose self-esteem was sufficiently high to understand and accept these revelations. But she hadn't. The marriage suffered from that moment on. Allen became terribly jealous and less loving. When the marriage ended in divorce two years later, Betty still did not understand what had happened.

Betty had taken her husband's interest as the normal curiosity of one friend for the activities of another. She was naive enough not to understand the male ego and self-esteem's relation to jealousy. She said, "I realized he wanted to marry a virgin, but a virgin that was super in bed . . . as if her knowledge came magically. He *knew* I wasn't a virgin. He even said he didn't *want* a virgin. But he didn't want me to be an "experienced" woman either. He couldn't accept the reality of it.

Betty realized the hard way that it's really important to understand one's own level of self-esteem, as well as that of your partner.

Elaine's and Jim's case may help illustrate the topic more effectively. Jim was nine years older than Elaine when they married on her 19th birthday. A perfect age difference, some say. Elaine had lived a sheltered life, first at home with parents in a small town, then in a restrictive religious high school and first year of college. But Elaine just could not buckle down to the college regime. Her mind wasn't on it.

Elaine's roommates were three sexually active girls, using much energy and wiles to get around the restrictions of the school to be with their boyfriends. They scoffed at Elaine's small-town ideas of remaining a virgin until marriage. "How are you going to know if you have a good man or not?" one asked her. "Unless you do a little sampling you will never know what you are missing."

Elaine dropped out of school and took a job as a secretary. Her boss was attractive, married and interested in his new office help. Still a virgin, Elaine decided to date her persistent boss. In the back of her mind, unadmitted to herself, was the idea that an older, more experienced man might show her the way. She dated her boss twice before she "allowed" herself to be seduced on her third date.

The affair with the boss lasted from that day until almost a year later when she met Jim. But she had not confined herself to just the sexual attentions of her boss because he could spare only one night a week, plus some rather awkward couplings after work. Elaine saw several other men and bedded all of them in a rather furious attempt to "catch up."

But after meeting Jim, she cut off all other male friends except for her boss, whom she still continued to see. She didn't know how to break it off with him, even though their relationship now was strictly sexual. But she felt that her boss had taught her much.

After Jim asked her to marry him, Elaine found the courage to break it off with her boss. She took the easiest way, that of quitting. Jim and Elaine were married some weeks later. Before the marriage and for some time afterwards, Elaine debated with herself about telling her happy new husband about her past. To her, her sexual history was quite lurid.

Although Elaine and Jim had had sex before they were married, it had been rather limited. This had been Elaine's desire and since it only seemed to heighten Jim's desire for her, she maintained this attitude even when she often did not wish to keep it up. But then she felt trapped. She had inadvertently given Jim the idea she was quite inexperienced, if not a virgin, or a "demi-virgin" as Jim had kidded her.

After a few months of marriage, Elaine began to worry. Her conscience began to trouble her. She thought she had given Jim a bad deal and since she loved him, she felt bad about it. He had the idea she was quite innocent and he seemed to hesitate to introduce her to any of the sex acts other than the simple, old-fashioned missionary position. Elaine, in her turn, couldn't bring herself to either admit she knew about these other things and in fact enjoyed them tremendously, or to allow him to introduce her to them.

These contradictory feelings increased Elaine's depressed mood. She went through days of listlessness, of moody, brooding periods that her husband thought were either disinterest in him sexually or dissatisfaction with their physical situation. Since he was working hard and giving her everything she wanted, he became resentful of her moods.

Elaine's housework became minimal and she grew listless. She began to think of nothing but the confrontation she felt she had to instigate. She saw her marriage falling apart and finally decided she had to tell Jim of her past life, that she was not the innocent near-virgin that he thought she was, and that she was really a lusty woman with deep sexual appetites which had been awakened by a married man.

Elaine hoped Jim was man enough with sufficiently high self-esteem and low jealousy; and that he loved her enough to understand and forgive what she believed was a lurid past.

Finally, one night, she got courage enough to tell Jim everything. When she was through he didn't say anything for some time. Then he began to question her. He asked for details, then more details, all of which were highly embarrassing to her. He became almost a prosecuting attorney, digging into details, demanding that she remember facts and feelings that had happened many months before. He kept probing deeper, asking for more details, more raw feelings.

Jim then started to ask her if perhaps she had forgotten some of her lovers, that perhaps she had left out a few. Elaine insisted that she had told him everything, that there were only a few and that she had told him everything. But Jim kept pounding away at her story, insisting on details, driving Elaine into tears and near-hysteria. At last, confused and frightened, she admitted that perhaps she had, indeed, forgotten a lover or two, for after all, you can't remember what you've forgotten.

Jim seized upon that point, drove her to tears, shouting at her, telling her she was a whore and was disgusting. He became angry enough to strike her, then he started packing to leave the house.

"I thought you would want to know," she said. "I thought you loved me enough to understand."

"You're a whore," he shouted at her. "How can I believe anything you say now???" "How can I make love to you now? I'd think about all those other men who fucked you first!"

Jim left the house. Their marriage was over. Although the divorce lawyer tried to talk them into seeing a marriage counselor, the marriage was not saved. (People seldom go to a marriage counselor until it's too late!)

Elaine later married a man with a high level of self-esteem to whom she had first explained everything, long before the marriage. Jim, she heard, had gone to the Phillipines, and had married a 16-year old certified virgin.

"It wasn't so much that he was hung up on virgins," Elaine said, "it was just that he didn't want a "used" wife. I guess there's a difference."

By confessing her imagined sins, by baring her sexual history to the wrong man, one with low self-esteem, Elaine had destroyed her marriage. She had felt guilty, first about the actual sex acts themselves, then about the accidental appearance of innocence she had given her husband. She was not strong enough to contain her guilt, to exorcise it, or to deal with it in any other way except to "dump" it on her husband.

Confession is sometimes used to pass the buck. You confess your sins to a priest, to God and he absolves you of the weight of your guilt. Elaine's confessions put the weight on a man who just couldn't handle it, because of his low self-esteem.

Confession is always to the good, if you are making revelations to a clergyman or a psychotherapist. It frees the confessing person from his/her guilt, but often adds to the burden of the innocent.

The jealous person's imagination is very active. It may take a few hints to build them into giant behemoths of ugliness, depravity, evil and anger. The confessional has been a major part of religions for centuries. But the confessor and the one who listens have an impersonal relationship. No ego or jealousy is involved. It works for the religious, but not the jealous. Many people are simply not able to cope with the reality of something when it differs from what they imagined it to be.

The higher your self-esteem, the less jealousy you will feel. Or, to put it the opposite way, **the higher your jealousy, the lower your self-esteem.**

Jealousy is a *complex emotion* that can include feelings of anger, grief, fear, suspicion and shame.

These more basic feelings are part of our humanity. Historically, they have survival value. Since "jealousy" itself is observable in primates other than man, it is possible that this more complex emotion also originated as a protective instinct. Instincts do not die easily, even when society has changed and they no longer have survival value.

Jealousy will not disappear, just because you want it gone. Let's look for just a moment at what jealousy really is. Jealousy is *not* **envy.** They are different not only in the relationships involved, but in the intensity of the feelings they cause. Envy usually concerns a relationship between two people; jealousy, three or more people. Envy is usually about things rather than people, but not always. You could be envious about a neighbor's mansion or Porsche. You might envy a friend because his partner makes charming conversation. He might envy you because your wife or husband makes a lot of money. You might envy a friend her good looks, charisma or apparently well educated children. She might envy you your lack of children. Envy is more passive than jealousy, wistful rather than grief-stricken, more pique than anger.

Jealousy and envy are both unpleasant emotions, but envy is like getting stung by a mosquito or, at worst, a bee. It hurts, but it is not overwhelming. Jealousy can be more like have a rusty jagged dagger shoved into your gut and — depending on the situation — slowly twisted. You rarely hear of people killing because of envy.

Feelings included with jealousy are fear, anticipated grief, insecurity and anger directed at the loved one or whoever is diverting his or her attentions. Usually, one or two of these components, like anger, may be felt more strongly. As such, jealousy always leads to feelings of low self-esteem. If persistent, jealousy directly lowers one's self-esteem.

From the beginning jealousy has always been recognized as bad. The Song of Solomon tells us, "Jealousy is as cruel as the grave."

> John Dryden called it: "Jaundice of the soul; tyrant of the mind."
> La Rochefoucauld: "more self-love than love."
> Thomas Middleton: "Wedlock's yellow sickness."
> John Milton: "The injured lover's hell."
> Johann C. Schiller: "The great exaggerator."
> William Shakespeare: "The green-eyed monster."
> Robert Louis Stevenson: "One of the consequences of love."
> Edward Young: "It is the hydra of calamities, the sevenfold death."

You may agree with one or more or all of the above. Regardless, there are various types of jealousy — sibling jealousy, professional jealousy, and social jealousy to name a few — but sexual jealousy is the one that affects most people most often. It seems to hurt the worst, as you may have already concluded from the real-life stories cited previously here in this chapter.

Asked what jealousy meant to her, a teacher said, "It basically boils down to two things with me. One, I'm feeling left out and I want to get involved with someone else. I want the sexual interchange that they're having. Or, I want to have him close so I feel like I'm not losing him. It's a fear of loss and a fear of being left out."

Almost all humans have felt this complex emotion. Clinical psychologists say almost everyone had experienced it, and those with low self-esteem surely suffer it most of all.

Your daily reading of the newspaper should convince you of humankind's *jealousy follies*. You will not be bored or excited here by the lurid recounting of all the penises cut off by jealous husbands or all the wayward husbands poisoned by their jealous wives.

Our research shows you can shrink your own "green-eyed monster." The effort you invest will be repaid you thousands of times during the rest of your life. You can accomplish a number of goals simultaneously. For example, as you work on reducing your jealousy, you also will be increasing your own self-esteem. It is possible to raise your over-all level of self-esteem to such a level that you will no longer experience feelings of jealousy. Or, if you do, you will be enabled to dissipate them very quickly.

Jealousy is one of those affective states, like grief, that may be described as normal. If anyone appears to be without it, the inference is justified that it has undergone severe repression and consequently plays all the greater part in his unconscious mental life. The instances of abnormally intense jealousy met with in analytic work reveal themselves as constructed of three layers. The three layers or stages of jealousy may be described as (1) competitive or normal; (2) projected; and (3) delusional jealousy.

Freud became convinced the pain of normal adult jealousy was really a re-opening of old psychic wounds first sustained in infancy. In competitive or normal jealousy, one feels grief-stricken over the loss or threatened loss of a loved one. Competitive jealousy is typically experienced in social situations like parties, which usually serve as ritual meeting grounds.

The second kind of jealousy, *projected jealousy*, has two components: (1) fantasies of being unfaithful to one's partner or the real experience of actual "unfaithfulness" and (2) the need to rationalize urges regarded as shameful or not allowed. An individual harassed with guilt from real or fanta-sized infidelity may resolve this guilt/conflict by attributing these "sins" to his/her partner. The subconscious dialogue becomes "I want to be with another person, but I can't accept this in myself. Therefore, I *accuse you* of wanting another lover." Or, "if I were my mate, I'd make love to that person. There-fore, (s)he must want to do the same." This process can be fairly complex, but the end result is accusing the lover of the very same things one has fantasized or actually committed. The old saying is "One does not look behind the door unless (s)he has stood there already."

Freud's third type of jealousy — delusional — is the most extreme example of this emotion. Delusional jealousy is based on clues that actually do not exist, except in the victim's mind. Psychotic individuals may have this type of pathological jealousy as part of their disturbed thought processes.

Paranoia is in part a reaction to insecurity, a defense mechanism gone haywire. The paranoid person is not just ever-alert but over-alert, frequently making false connections and interpretations. Paranoids are over-alert to love rivals and inordinately jealous because they're desperately trying to defend against the insecurity the loss of a loved one represents. Like all jealous lovers, they graphically imagine sexual contact with the real or imagined love rival. But they're more frequently and more unreasonably jealous than most people because of their extreme insecurity and grossly disturbed thought processes.

"*Crazy*"people may experience a lot of jealousy; but you're not necessarily psychotic just because you feel jealous (though people in its grip have wondered about temporary insanity).

Jealousy itself is no more abnormal than anger, joy or grief. You're possibly reading this now because you or someone you know experiences jealousy too frequently or intensely. If you believe these words are really coded messages to your lover, they may not help resolve your problem. Otherwise, you're on the path to understanding and controlling these perplexing feelings.

Your Jealousy Escape-Package

Here is a ten-fold list of goals to set for yourself. Understand, set them, and continuously act upon them.

(1) **Admit your jealous feelings.** You may feel ashamed or guilty about having these feelings. This is one of the great double-binds or Catch-22's of our life. Don't wallow in guilt. Be good to yourself by using all the other methods outlined in this book. If you deny it, you are literally doomed to be constantly a green-eyed monster. Accept it as a valid emotion, as a normal part of growth, as a path to greater understanding. Self-acceptance is a key to greater self-esteem. Don't slide into bitter self-criticism.

(2) **Retreat/Escape.** The best escape is to retreat. Take a short break — across the street, across town, or across the country, depending on your situation. Naturally, you can't always run away from the pain. But you should physically remove yourself from the place where you experienced traumatic events.

(3) **Talk out your feelings.** Find someone empathetic, understanding, accepting and willing to listen. Avoid someone who might secretly enjoy your pain. Avoid a casual acquaintance who merely mouths: "Don't be jealous." One immediate result may be that you see your fears are not valid. If you can't find an amateur friend, then hurry to a professional friend, your local friendly psychotherapist.

(4) **Exercise and sleep.** A hot bath, sauna, or a swim first may help. Perhaps you can find a friend to give you a great massage. If you can exercise first, your sleep may be doubly rewarding and may help restore your psychological equilibrium.

(5) **Write out your feelings.** Put your emotions on paper. Organize your jealousy as fully and carefully as possible. Don't hesitate to state your actual fears of rejection, of loss, of loneliness; your anger, resentment, competitiveness, rejection, and the like. You may find it easier to put it into a letter — which you will *not* mail. You will be amazed at how much you learn about yourself.

(6) **Meditate on your jealousy.** Consciously relax your body by all the methods described earlier in this book, in the chapter about self-hypnosis. Deliberately think about the character and depth of all those painful feelings, until you can sense a difference between you, yourself, and those feelings. "Here I am," and "There are *those* feelings." Ask yourself: "Is this pain so insufferable? Is it truly that painful?" It is painful alright! But you will find that this meditative separation of feelings permits you to understand with greater clarity that it's not the end of the world. You will survive. You will become an

even bigger winner. Apply all in the Self-Affirmation portion of the chapter on Self-Hypnosis.

The great advantage of this exercise is that, instead of allowing jealousy to hound you in the guise of a vaguely defined menace, you are deliberately setting aside time to face the beast head-on. By confronting the green-eyed monster, you undercut its power over you.

As you complete the exercise, tell yourself: "Okay. I've given it my full attention. I've looked at it squarely. Now, I can put it out of my mind for a while."

If jealousy invades your mind when you're *not* doing this exercise, remember you've made an appointment with yourself to think about it at another time. You are not running from your feelings, but learning to deal with them on your terms at your convenience. Do this exercise three times a day for just a few minutes. (Use it also for any other feelings, such as anger, that you may choose to work on and eliminate).

(7) **Keep busy = Don't "worry" too much.** Use the goal setting methods described earlier in this book to root out any negative thought, or emotion. If you fall into the trap of worry, you will occupy all your time embroidering endless answers to countless questions. You can get unbelievably worked up improvising the most elaborate scenarios. It's like starring in your own horror movie, and regardless of the ending, you lose:

Here are some things you can do:

(A) Work out physically.
(B) Paint a room.
(C) Rearrange furniture.
(D) Play a game you enjoy.
(E) See a good film — one *not* about jealousy.
(F) Cook a great meal.
(G) Anything else that seems to work for you.

(8) **Read books of wisdom.** There are many great self-help books around. Any book about your personal growth and development will help you focus on positive issues rather than permit you to succumb to negativism. This includes using all the other methods in the present book on increasing your self-esteem.

(9) **Laugh.** Please read the chapter in this book on how humor will enable you to feel better. Laughter is one of the best ways to deal with jealousy. It will prevent you from taking yourself too seriously. Go to a funny movie or a comedy club to hear a comedian. Watch a sitcom on TV.

(10) **Keep these ten points with you.** Make up a short list of these ten methods and put them in your wallet/purse. Then look at them and do them regularly.

Prevent Future Jealousy

Jealousy can become part of a vicious circle, because, like cancer, jealousy feeds on itself. The more jealous you are, the lower your self-esteem. And then, the more you feel low in self-esteem, the more likely you will be to feel jealous. The opposite is also true: the more you work on increasing your positive feelings of self-esteem, the less likely you will feel jealous in the future.

A valid sense of self-esteem will help you distinguish between true and false fears of loss. You have seen how jealousy can distort your rational thinking. Jealousy *feels* the same whether based on valid threats or not. It is so powerful that many efforts to confront it head-on seem useless. Thus, you need to use all the other methods in this book to increase your self-esteem.

Here are some additional ways to prevent jealousy in the future, by working more directly on your self-esteem.

(1) **High self-esteem people view the world as a friendly place.** How do you look at your surroundings? Does it seem hospitable or hostile? You can choose the way you view reality. Set goals directly to perceive the world as an opportunity for stimulation, information, joy and future happiness.

(2) **High self-esteem people view others as basically benevolent.** How do you regard others who dwell in your world? You probably see very well by now that their interactions with you depend on how you respond to them first. Fewer facial muscles are needed to smile than to frown. The quality of your encounters reflects what you emanate from within yourself. You may have heard these ideas before, but it's easy to forget.

(3) **High self-esteem people tend toward optimism.** How do you believe things will work out for you? At work? In your relationships? Children? Family? If you assume and predict things will go well, you have a greater chance of success. It is just as easy to make a positive self-fulfilling prophesy, as it is to predict failure, a negative self-fulfilling prophesy. You can keep in touch with reality through a positive attitude. Positive thinking has proven to be very powerful.

(4) **High self-esteem people tend to be relaxed and stable.** All elements in your home, family, work, relationships and health should each include feelings of ease, calm, security and satisfaction. If you do not feel as great as you want, examine each single element or factor and set goals to change them. There are so many methods described in this book and elsewhere, to aid you in achieving a calm, relaxed attitude. Choose those appropriate for you.

(5) **High self-esteem people want to be outgoing and take an interest in others.** Remember all the hellos, smiles and "warm fuzzies" — the positive psychological strokes you can give others. You can enrich your own life immeasurably when you invest in the lives of others — family, friends or strangers. Find a social cause you can support that will give purpose and meaning to your life. You need not be overly extroverted to develop a sense of community. Remember the NASA space pictures of our earth as a space ship among galaxies.

(6) **High self-esteem people are self-accepting.** You are okay as you are now. This does not go against your goals to maintain and increase your

present inner strengths. You already possess admirable, strong qualities, if you have been around long enough to read this book.

(7) **High self-esteem people tend to be happy.** The highway to happiness is indirect. Happiness is a side-effect of other facts of life that are satisfying. Although you cannot achieve happiness directly, you can reflect on activities in your life that have produced previous joys. Use them as guide-posts for your conduct.

(8) **High self-esteem people feel loved.** They own a sense of belong-ingness, of togetherness and believe others regard them with warmth. You feel much stronger when you are surrounded by people you care for, who can also love you in return. Set goals to search out more loving people. But be aware of joining for the sake of joining—groups led by charismatic con-artists.

(9) **High self-esteem people have learned to resolve conflicts.** You can avoid win-lose situations, because you can turn them into win-win events. You can have two bigger winners, instead of two losers; because, if you have one winner and one loser, you still have two losers. Clarify your goals. By reducing conflicts in your goals and relationships, you will enhance your feelings of self-esteem.

(10) **High self-esteem people have learned valuable coping skills.** You can set goals to risk and learn new skills of relating. You can be optimistic, treat others kindly, be loving and loved, relaxed, outgoing, happy, and still realistically live in the real world.

Chapter 11

Guilt

Perry came to SECS to see a sex therapist because he was impotent. The therapist was amazed to hear Perry state he'd been married for seven years. *Both* he and his wife were *still* virgins.

Perry had been a childhood victim of incest. He slept with his widowed mother until he realized incest was happening. Perry ran away at age fifteen.

Ever since he has been unable and unwilling to engage in any sexual activities. The more Perry sobbed out his story, the more he realized **guilt** was part of his problem.

Many people in our society *today*, have experienced deep guilt feelings about love and sex, regardless of the cause.

Religion has always been one of the great **guilt**-inducing forces in life. We are *not* here today to blame or exonerate religious leaders but to help you understand more about guilt. As you learn more about guilt, then you will have a better opportunity to avoid it. **Entertaining guilt feelings** is one of the most obvious ways to lower your self-esteem.

What is Guilt?

Guilt is like the common cold. Everyone gets it, everyone has much to say about it. But what *can* you do to prevent it or rid yourself of it?

Psychologists agree, everybody feels guilty. If there is one absolute in life, it is that. Most of us walk around much of the time feeling guilty about something.

The type of guilt most people feel is not reserved for criminals or dirty-tricksters. Rather, it is of the nit-picky, everyday garden variety. It is unnecessary guilt.

Because unnecessary guilt suffuses the total fabric of our lives, many can't imagine life without it. During a recent TV show, the interviewer asked a famous Hollywood actor if he didn't feel guilty about his gambling.

The actor-gambler replied that he had lived all his life with guilt and anxiety, so much so that he felt very uneasy in their absence. He felt similar to the New Yorker transplanted to clean, crisp, pollution-free air of the high-Rockies of Colorado. He felt "very nervous" because he could not see the air he was supposed to breathe.

Although most of us are "used-to" guilt, not everyone considers it a valued friend. But if it is an old friend, it's more like the kind who comes to your house for a weekend visit and ends up moving in with you, lock, stock and barrel. Old friend or not, you really feel relieved when he gets it together to move out.

Guilt is the relentless feeling standing between most of us and our dream of having a little *real* relaxation, a little *real* pleasure, a little *real* peace of mind.

Libraries have been written about guilt by theologians, therapists, and philosophers. You could also fill libraries with poems, novels and plays where the main theme is guilt. *Guilt* is a continuing fight between you and *yourself*. For some people, it is the "sense of original sin." Or your feeling you deserve to be punished. The *American Heritage Dictionary* defines guilt as "Remorseful awareness of having done something wrong."

With a little mental effort, a guilt habit that has been built up over many years can be changed. All those daily doses of guilt that we get from such divergent sources as accountants, dental receptionists, head waiters, parents, friends, bosses, lovers, the government, the *world*, and yes, even animals can be handled successfully and avoided.

"I feel guilty about everything," said Jerry, a thirty year old systems analyst. "I can't help it. I worry about everything, and when anything goes wrong, I always blame myself. Even when I'm blaming someone else about it, I'm thinking inside that some way, somehow, it's really all my fault. Then, of course, I feel twice as guilty afterward. Even my guilt has guilt."

Hidden Guilt

Early in childhood we formed guilt-ridden feelings and attitudes that remain with us most of our lives, unless we actively work to change them. Many of these feelings seem fairly harmless, and in fact are not even recognized for what they are by people who harbor them.

Hidden guilt is very difficult to eradicate because it is often disguised as another emotion. It comes in different varieties as indicated in the following examples.

Mary absolutely refuses to watch soap operas on TV. Not that she dislikes them. Secretly, she adores them. But everyone in her crowd puts them down. She won't turn them on even when she's *alone*, fearing her friends would not approve. Mary is projecting a fear into the future, and also feeling guilty because of her best friends' *non approval.*

Tom refuses to go into a fast food chain for a quick burger and shake. Suppose somebody from his office saw him going in there, instead of the usual lunch places they frequent. He puts himself down because he knows that sometimes what he really craves is a Whopper of a Big Mac. Could you believe a Big Mac attack induces so much guilt?? After all, real men do not eat Quiche!

Jim changes from his faded jeans and T-shirt into a three piece suit before he goes to visit his parents. He hates himself for doing it, but can't permit himself to see what he looks like most of the time. Because he feels so miserable, he is sullen and angry during dinner, which only makes them criticize him more.

Harry's girlfriend wants him to quit smoking, but he can't. Instead, he smokes the "light beige" brand she suggested. Because he hates the new brand, he slowly smokes twice as many in defiant anger.

All of us are sensitive to the likes and dislikes of people around us. But you don't want to carry a good thing too far. Denying yourself pleasures because of what someone else thinks or likes definitely will lower your self-esteem, and at the same time it will flame hidden fires of anger toward them. You are really harming yourself most of all. Little self-denials add up until you have hundreds, enough in fact so that you no longer have any genuine pleasures left. Or if you have one left, you feel guilty about it. As a victim of hidden guilt, you feel more and more miserable, more and more uncomfortable in your skin, until life seems hardly worth living. You wonder what is wrong, without ever suspecting the cause to be hidden guilt over your own simple preferences and choices in life.

Guilt and Family

"Guilt?" grimaces a young woman writer. "I'll give you my mother's phone number. She'll tell you everything you need to know. But watch out. The first thing she'll do is make you feel guilty about calling her up in the first place."

Regardless of how guilty your mother may make you feel, you might feel better realizing someone else always has a better horror story. It helps to remember that no matter how old you get, your parents will never forget the days before you were toilet trained, or the years when they were the only people you could turn to for help and advice.

Facing up to the fact that they may *never* be able to fully approve of your lifestyle is one way to cope with the guilt they subtly, or not so subtly, make you feel.

Many children experience lifelong guilt caused by parents who are simply not very nice people. It never occurs to them that their mothers and fathers are not kind, selfless people. Others are also surprised to learn that they can continue to *love* a parent without actually *liking* the way they behave or the way they make them feel.

"I always expected my mother to be perfect," said Josh, "and I wasted years feeling angry with her because she obviously wasn't. Then, I'd always feel really bad, really guilty about the things I'd been feeling about her. It was really some kind of illumination, you know, flash-bulb variety, when I realized, 'my God, this woman isn't perfect.' Why should she be, just because she's my mother."

Guilt and Health

Guilt-ridden people may be unable to express their true feelings for fear of showing their imperfections to others. But only a moment's reflection will reveal the "astounding" idea that we're all in the same shape as far as perfection is concerned. Realizing this allows you to relax a little bit more, conceding your fears and imperfections. Many people permit themselves to feel guilty about having fears, as if others did not. Imagine you are riding in a car with a drunken driver pushing 80 miles an hour. Would you really rather die than risk exposing your fears??

Obviously, feelings of guilt can harm us and others. Such physical manifestations as ulcers have long been associated with unnecessary feelings of guilt. Psychosomatic illnesses of all varieties are caused by people who suppress their feelings rather than learning to express them correctly. The oft discussed hangover has been linked with yet another form of guilt. One reason you may feel so bad the morning after is that you *think* you *ought* to feel bad. Having a good time, especially with alcohol, doesn't fit in with the traditions by which most Americans are raised. Guilt may explain why disgusting cures like raw eggs and Tobasco seem to work. The concept of paying for a good time is as old as the hills. Fortunately, most of us have progressed beyond the need to sleep on a bed of nails or wear a hair shirt simply because we are creatures clearly in need of pleasures.

For some it is a bitter struggle just to eke out a bit of pleasure for themselves without feeling guilty about it. Jeff, a twenty-six year old CPA put it this way: "I actually have to force myself to do something good for myself each day." Jeff was so repressed that he would feel guilty about buying himself a pair of socks he really needed, or a new tie he could surely afford. Through therapy he realized what he was doing or not doing to himself. He could finally set goals to reduce guilt and increase his self-esteem.

Rewarding yourself just *because* you exist is the first step toward fighting feeling guilty just because you exist.

Guilt and Work

"In TV ads, all vacationers look very ecstatic," said Frank, a midwestern attorney. "When I'm on vacation, I'm really miserable." A surprising number of people find it impossible to relax, even during their well-earned vacation time.

"All my life I've been taught there is something sacred about work, something that will turn us into some kind of saint," says Ellen, a twenty-eight year old banker. "All I get from work is tired."

"I am incapable of lying down on a beach blanket to get a tan, unless I had with me a book to improve my mind, pens and paper to respond to letters I've been feeling guilty about all year, and a pad to make notes about things I should do back home," says Jim, a Chicago tax specialist.

"The popularity of Zen and Yogic centers and courses in this country is partially due to a national need to learn how to sit and do nothing," suggests Janet, a Minnesota Yoga teacher. "It is the hardest thing for most Americans and many Europeans who have caught up with our 'modern' way of life to do." Learning not to feel guilt about just "sitting" is a major step to increasing your self-esteem.

Guilty Workaholics are prey to an enormous amount of stress. Researchers suggest that the trick to handling it is to find the stress level where you function best and then to try avoiding any further anxieties. One way to relax is to provide definite breathing spaces during the day, without allowing yourself to feel guilty about it.

Work relationships are frequently bound up in guilt. Some bosses find themselves in positions of greater authority via the "Peter Principle." The "Peter Principle" is the observation made by Lawrence Peter in his book of that title (Morrow) that most people are promoted to the position just above the level at which they have the most competence. In other words, when you're really good at something, chances are you'll get promoted to a job you're not so good at. A person who has "earned" a position of higher authority through seniority may know that someone under him is actually better at his job than *he* is. It would be unusual to have a person in such a position refuse a promotion, or step down, saying, "Listen, you take over. You're obviously better at this job." But what does happen is that the higher-up experiences a serious case of guilt (often not admitted to himself) about the employee.

Guilt that persons in authority feel via the "Peter Principle," or from other sources, is usually laid on everyone in the office by making them feel guilty about something. It may show up in nit-pickiness about unimportant details, paying undue attention to length of coffee breaks, tardiness, and the like.

A constant awareness about guilt feelings, particularly in business, is necessary to stay healthy and to lighten the burden of work. Recognition is a first step to reduce guilt feelings and make necessary decisions to change the patterns that cause it. Admitting guilt feelings is an important step toward increasing self-esteem.

Guilt, The Wolf in Sheep's Clothing

Guilt is often a disguise for many other feelings. The trick is to recognize the true feelings underneath and to deal with *those.* Trying to cope with guilt without knowing what lies beneath it is like wrestling with a wolf in sheep's clothing. But if you are aware of what you are dealing with, your fighting tactics are bound to become more effective.

Researchers estimate that at least 60 percent of unnecessary guilt can be reduced simply by understanding why we feel guilty and realizing you are not alone (we all tend to feel guilty about similar things).

Once you get the hang of discovering entirely different feelings submerged beneath your "guilt," you've already gone a long way toward ridding yourself of the unnecessary kinds of guilt that can make your life miserable.

Here are some examples of various emotional states that can masquerade as guilt:

Anger. Rob's boss knows he's not feeling well, but asks him to stay late to finish a project anyway. Rob refuses, begging out of it tactfully. On the way home, even though he's sick, he feels guilty for not staying. His basic emotion is anger that Old Fuddy-Duddy had the gall to ask him to stay. Going with the anger, admitting it to himself (though he may not let the boss know it) can alleviate Rob's unnecessary guilt. It will surely make Rob feel better, too.

Ego Inflation. Jack declares he feels guilty taking even one day off from work even if he's really sick. But he really can't accept the thought that things at work might go on well without him. Unnecessary guilt masks his need to be in constant control of everything.

Timidity. Heather says yes to almost everything that is asked of her from typing a friend's homework to having sex. The unnecessary guilt she feels before she says yes is due to her lack of assertiveness. The guilt she feels afterward is anger at her inability to control her life. Recognizing both hidden emotions will help her say no more often, without feeling guilt.

Fear. Marianna feels unnecessary guilt if the least thing goes awry in the household she shares with Johnny. Even though they both work, she feels she must be a perfect cook and housekeeper as well as someone who can bring home a paycheck. Caught in the middle of ERA/Women's lib, Marianna's guilt masks her unrealistic goal of being absolutely perfect in all things and to all people (a perfect old fashioned homemaker). Her fear is that she will lose her man if she cannot live up to both these ideals. Recognizing this will help her discuss it with him and make life easier for herself and consequently for both of them.

Desire. Al feels guilty whenever his lover's best friend Terri is around. He becomes rude and distant with both of them, without really understanding why. He feels guilty afterward. He is uneasy about the attraction he felt for Terri when he first met her, and he turned his emotion into one of dislike, because he had no intention of being unfaithful to his girlfriend. By accepting his original feelings of desire (even though he need not act upon them), Al could save himself and his girlfriend a lot of grief.

Boredom. Ted and Karen spend a lot of time seeing old friends, a couple they've known since high school. They'd feel guilty not keeping up the relationship, and consequently put a lot of time and energy into it. But Ted and Karen are basically bored with these people. They'd do themselves and their friends a favor by slowly dropping the relationship.

Sexual Guilt

Here, consider just one kind of guilt — sexual guilt. You may imagine sexual guilt as a very hot, humid dark jungle, with the blood-curdling screeches of ferocious hidden animals, odors of perfume and decay, a mix of danger and desire. Sex therapists and psychologists do not see guilt as mysterious or romantic. The more correct comparison would be an old, wet blanket.

Feeling guilty keeps you from jumping for joy or pulsing with pleasure. Guilt creates chasms between *You* and *Now*. You can't be here now, when you worry what you should or should not do.

You become reluctant to ask for or suggest a change of pace or position. You can't state "more" or "less," "harder" or "softer," "faster or slower." Sexual guilt prevents your sharing more interesting, involved ideas about sex.

Guilt really puts you down. It makes you feel less a human being. Sexual guilt literally makes you hide inside the cave-like coffin of what you expect that others expect of you.

Nothing turns better pleasure *more* sour than sexual guilt. You can view it as a form of anxiety that causes passionate women to avoid desire and strong men to lose erections.

Sexual guilt can rob intimacy from love-making and makes sex impersonally mechanical, if it can be done at all. Just as you learned sexual guilt in the first place, now you can *unlearn* it. You no longer have to live with it now, even if you've always remembered it. You can throw off that dirty, dark, wet blanket today. You'll be amazed at how much better the world looks.

Freedom from guilt is the great feeling you can have — of being your own wonderful self.

People have an uncanny ability to feel guilty about anything. In my role as a former Roman Catholic priest who had to listen to confessions for seven years in all kinds of parishes and cathedrals, I was constantly amazed at the wide range of guilt. A little 8 year old girl once blurted out: "I fighted with my older sister, I fighted with my younger sister. And I fighted with my middle sister..." Then after a long sigh she whispered, "And I sweared." You might want to respond, as I did, but somehow managed to hold it all back: "Listen little girl, your problem is not guilt...it's your grammar."

The whole gamut of human experience can make people feel guilty. Sexual guilt has been experienced by all kinds of people over simple loving behaviors like touching themselves, touching others, sexual pleasures, fantasies about movies and TV stars or even making love with the lights on.

Here's a brief list of some ideas that often cause people to feel sexual guilt:

- Since sex is only for marriage, what I'm doing is shameful and wrong.
- If it's pleasurable, it has to be sinful.
- If I try oral sex or masturbate or have fantasies about extramarital sex, something really bad will happen to me.
- "Nice" girls shouldn't do these awful things.
- I should be doing more useful things than wasting my time doing sexy, bad things.
- I shouldn't enjoy this so...

You cannot feel good about yourself or even sexy if you feel guilty. The guilt you feel is directly proportional to the pleasure you don't feel.

Joyless sex is pandemic (or for some an unfortunate epidemic). There's so much hope and so much greater disappointment. Sex occurs without tenderness, passion, joy or fun. Sex without love is very prevalent. Shame and guilt in our parents or other teachers forced them to teach sex only for procreation. It's almost as if parents and teachers teamed up with pornographers to view sex as just genital friction. Joyless sex is one good reason to unlearn guilt.

Jesus said: "what good does it do if you gain the whole world but suffer the loss of your immortal soul?" To paraphrase Him: "What good is it to you to make love, but not enjoy it? Or what good is to to you to make *nonlove*. Or what good is it to you if you do not experience life and love? Then you haven't lived."

How You Learned to Feel Guilty about Love and Sex

The eerie feeling that sex is shameful comes from even the most generous, considerate and loving parents. Some parents tell children sex is dirty or just a duty. (One client told me her mother responded to sex-queries by saying: "It happens while you're asleep." As if some demonic incubus descended upon her from hell and impregnated her with a monster.)

Too many parents are silent about sex. In their silence, they teach us sex by default. But "default" lies with them. These parents do not teach us that we are sexual beings. Masters and Johnson and other have constantly reminded us we must learn to accept sex as a natural function. Just like brushing teeth or combing your hair. Parents do not display enough loving between themselves. So the most important role-models in our lives have missing parts.

Thousands of children grow up thinking if there are three kids, then their parents did it three times. In your home, chances are that wars, politics, baseball, basketball, soap operas, cars, high school clothes, were all open for discussion — all except sex. In that environment, you know you have something to hide. Were you caught touching yourself??? **Shame, shame, shame!!!** Putting *tabu* perfume on your taboo body? Shame on you . . . You will burn in hell forever. You are guilty of a monstrous crime. Sex is bad: therefore it must be saved for your loved one in marriage. Isn't that an irony? Usually you only save good things for your loved ones. Imagine getting caught redhanded so to speak. You are lying on your bed in your room, very secretly masturbating. Your mother just happens to stroll in — it's the worst crime of your life. Bad enough to do it — but to get caught!!!

Masturbation is basic to your sexual self . . . and to your future loving self. It is probably your first and for many years your only sexual experience. Guilt felt by most men about masturbation is one specific, direct cause of one typical male sexual difficulty — premature ejaculation. Because more men masturbate furtively and guiltily, and all too hurriedly, and because they feel such deep shame at the same time, then the sooner it's all over the less chance they have of getting caught. (You really have to experience it to understand what it feels like.) So millions of men grew up being conditioned to ejaculate too quickly. Every male client I treated for premature ejaculation revealed a history of hurried, guilt-ridden masturbation. As a result, sex therapists and sexual surrogates have to teach men to slow down and prolong their masturbation. And naturally, they will greatly increase their pleasure and peace of mind.

Similarly, most women who have never experienced an orgasm have never masturbated, either because of a lack of information or guilt. In fact, one primary way women can learn to experience orgasm is by masturbating. Humans are especially endowed with a great capacity for pleasure — and they can learn to increase it. Masturbation really is a fine pleasure. For example, a woman's clitoris has nothing to do with procreation directly. It's only function is to give pleasure. Only women have an organ that is designed *only* for pleasure. (See how lucky you are?)

Sex and Religion

Sex and God are not poles apart. Only sex and religion have recently become poles apart. Parish priests since the dark and middle ages have taught young people to confess their "sins" of masturbation. Just as the priests themselves were taught how to whip themselves as penance so that they could fight off the blue demons of temptation. Because religious denominations taught us in part that we are born in sin, some want you to believe that the love of pleasure is antithetical to the love of God. Nothing could be further from the truth.

If God did not want you to enjoy pleasure, for example of masturbating or sucking on a woman's clitoris, why would he have designed it so beautifully in the first place???

Just as religion can be one of the major sources of sexual guilt, it can also be one of the major means of *relief from guilt.*

This dilemma or paradox is easily explained by Christianity. Many early Church writers were ultra-strict. St. Augustine was a fifth century ascetic who insisted that "original sin" (of Adam and Eve) causes sexual pleasure to lead people from God. Sex was **not** for pleasure but **only** to create life and only between husband and wife.

Many modern theologians take a much more liberal view. More than a few Catholic scholars now put it this way: "Sexual pleasure is a gift of God. It does *not* require any other purpose, if it draws you outside of selfish needs and into involvement with another human being."

Protestant theologians phrase it simply this way: "Let's begin with love. Is sex loving??? Sex should not be put into categories like right or wrong; good or bad; liberating or confining. Rather, is it loving? Each situation is unique. You make your own decisions, based on your *own* values, the values you put on marriage, intimacy, on others and on yourself."

Jewish Rabbis explained it this way: "For Jews, sex is a blessing. They have been instructed to read the Song of Songs before going to bed on the Sabbath. It is an extremely erotic poem. For thousands of years, the Hebrew tradition has encouraged the love art. The Sabbath is supposed to be devoted to rest, to reinvigorate the body, and also the soul. It is a day of love. In the Talmud and in the Old Testament, Judaism makes a strong statement against celibacy and for love. The Rabbis of the Talmud encouraged the many varieties of the loving act. For the Jew, sin is failure to make full use of the gifts God has given. One of the most obvious of God's gifts is sex."

Despite their different backgrounds, many theologians agree that God's word as expressed in the Bible and the Talmud literally celebrates sexuality and invites you to join in the celebration. Sexual pleasure is one of the most incomparably magnificent affirmations of life, and of one's own self-esteem.

Sex involves important responsibilities that need to be taught, but not at the risk of inducing more harmful *guilt.* Sex should not hurt anyone by being impersonal, exploitative or not intimate. That leads to harmful tragedies.

Sex obviously can lead to pregnancy. Thus, you and your partner should appreciate and share responsibilities for contraception or conception.

The essential issue here is that sexual fun involves responsibility — contraceptive responsibility and emotional responsibility. It's one of the most important obligations that you cannot avoid, even if you decide to spend one quick tryst in bed.

How to Unlearn Guilt

Imagine that Shakespeare has put Hamlet on his therapist's couch: "Where, oh, where does this guilt come from? From my dead father or my revered mother? Why this quiet that makes fungus of my passion, open sores of my love? Why, oh, why am I guilty??"

We suggest you try our couch instead. Most sex therapy clients really do *not* understand how guilt affects them. They are unaware how guilt influences their everyday thoughts and feelings about sex. Most people with sexual problems caused by guilt do not readily see just *how* their guilt is related to their religious upbringing. **Expecting to feel guilty and not wanting to feel guilty** keeps people from giving and receiving love and affection.

Guilt is a feeling you learn. Since you have *learned* to feel sexual guilt, you can also *unlearn* it. You can also, happily, unlearn it without being forced to or choosing to unlearn other values. That is, you can still love Motherhood, apple pie and the flag without at the same time feeling guilty about sex. You need *not* become "loose" or "chaste" to reduce your feelings of guilt. You may still retain the values you do **value now.** Now, however, you can learn to keep them out of a renewed sense of their importance rather than out of guilt.

To unlearn guilt, you need to shuck off other people's programming of your sexual feelings. Then you can be free to be creative and confident of your feelings. You will want to and will be able to be freer to choose according to your own values. Then you can thoroughly enjoy your own beauty and pleasure. Psychologist Albert Willis has written eloquently about "Too Much Masturbation" and about the "Tyranny of Should and Ought."

The main point is that to increase your self-esteem and improve all facets of your life, you need to learn how to lead your *own* life. I cannot, for example, lead my dad's life for him as a junior version of his values.

The first method to unlearn guilt is at the basis of behavior therapy, "graduated calming," or "desensitization." It was initially researched by Dr. Joseph Wolpe, pioneer of behavior therapy. He noticed that negative emotions of guilt cancel out positive feelings such as joy, love and pleasure. The reverse is also true. If you feel deeply relaxed or highly sexual, you do not experience guilt. Here is how it all happens:

Wolpe observed "graduated calming" is re-learning on a neurological and emotional level. It leads you slowly, step by step, up a ladder (or "hierarchy") of the things that make you anxious. As you quiet each smaller anxiety, your bigger feelings of anxiety become less intense.

You start with any happy emotional state, sexual excitement or relaxation. Then, you imagine an event or scene that causes you to experience anxiety. Then you return to the positive state of relaxation or erotic excitement. In other words, you will only *very* gradually, step-by-step, approach whatever it is that makes you feel guilty. You continuously get closer and closer. But you never get near enough to feel guilty at the same time as you remain sufficiently relaxed or sexually excited to feel pleasure and calm. With repetition and a graduated, systematic approach, a new learning takes place.

You begin to confront *without* guilt what used to inflame guilt. And you unlearn guilt you used to feel. Here's a quick and easy method. Draw up a list of things that make you feel sexually guilty. Then take just one concern on your list, break it down into its various points. Then make up a hierarchy with zero being total relaxation and one hundred being complete panic. (Later on, you can choose another item and repeat the process).

When you feel you are at the zero point, relaxed and sexually aroused with no guilt feelings, do the very lowest thing on your scale. Whenever you feel the slightest discomfort, uneasiness or guilt, just stop. Then, return to doing something that will cause you to feel sensual and erotic, until your discomfort is lowered. Please wait until your uneasiness is lowered to zero before you make your next attempt.

Whenever you can make the first step without feeling any discomfort or guilt, move up to the very next step on your ladder. You can take as much time as you need to work up your ladder, just as any Tibet mountain climber might do. The whole idea is to go slowly one step at a time.

Here is a nudity hierarchy, for example, of any woman who feels too thin, too bony, too fat, or too ugly:

Therapeutic Hierarchy

0	Lie in bed, relaxed in panties and bra
20	Lie in bed under covers nude with partner
30	Lie in bed nude with partner, lights off and no covers
50	Lights on, slowly taking off bra and panties
70	Lights on, lying naked next to partner
80	Walk around the room nude
100	Lover aroused, admiring her body

After your hierarchy is finished, the next step is to feel erotic. Use your favorite fantasy, sexy pictures or magazines to reach a fairly strong arousal level. You will need more arousal to stop a little guilt. But a "little" guilt is all you need to conquer, at each step in the process. You can keep improving on your hierarchy. As you move the first item down from 20 to zero, you can move all the other items down the scale. After you overcome the item numbered as ten, then you move the previous number 20 down to a 10. The most effective method to reduce guilt is this gradual, direct calming or "desensitization." Two others are "thought-stopping" and "assertive dialogues."

Thought-Stopping

Whenever an ancient, typical guilty thought or idea drifts into your mind, you need to immediately close it out. Stop it by silently emphasizing "**stop**" to yourself and replace it with any thought that is happy, positive, optimistic, and constructive. (Examples: "It's a mortal sin to touch yourself down there!" Father McHugh, rest his soul, would not give me absolution for this!" "Enjoying yourself is a terrible way to squandor time." "Mother and Dad would *just die* if they knew...")

Thought stopping is very easy to learn how to do. It requires little or no effort, once you get the hang of it. If you happen to be engaged in any sexual activity, you can substitute the guilt-producing thought by filling your mind with the physical pleasures you are feeling. All you need to do is learn to focus a little more or concentrate on the correct ideas and not the wrong ones.

Assertive — Dialogues

To deal with religious guilt, assertive dialogues are very effective. If you feel guilty about using birth control methods (because your church is against contraception) and you wish to conquer that, you could engage in an imaginary conversation.

Priest: "It's a mortal sin to use contraception."

You: "Yes, correct, Father! I know it is."

Priest: "You must know that the Roman Catholic Church for centuries has taught it is the most serious kind of mortal sin."

You: "Yes, Father, I do know. But I have thought about it seriously. My conscience tells me it is moral for me."

Priest: "Are you willing to risk your immortal soul for a moment's fleeting pleasure?"

You: "I must follow my conscience. How could that ever by sinful?"

One of your possible reactions might be that these three easy methods look too simple to solve the entire problem of guilt. The beauty of it is that these three methods really are very simple and also *work*. You can quickly reduce your sexual guilt and increase your pleasure.

People used to believe — falsely — that medicine had to taste terrible and require too long to work properly. Now, you can learn how to be free from guilt and anxiety. You can improve your life and your self-esteem today. You can begin now, and **you can succeed**....

Final Checklist to Reduce Unnecessary Guilt

1. Remind yourself constantly of all your good qualities as often as possible, even if it initially makes you feel uneasy to do so.
2. List all things (people, events, ideas) that you feel most guilty about. Do this daily until you can face each one point by point. Then develop new ways of looking at these hang ups.
3. Take more initiatives in relationships that are guilt-producing, rather than letting them run you.

4. Realize when your expectations of others are unrealistic. Most changes for the better come from you, not others. (Blaming another person for making you feel guilty will only stop when *you* stop feeling guilty.)

5. Before you start feeling guilty about what another person thinks, understand what their real feelings actually are. Frequently, they couldn't care less about something you inwardly torment yourself about.

6. Avoid over extending yourself (taking on jobs you cannot comfortably perform; agreeing to render services that make your life overly difficult). Offer honest explanations for refusing. The truer your explanation, the less guilt you will feel and the more understanding and accepting the other person is likely to be.

7. Learn to accept your own minor character flaws, or set goals to change them.

8. Avoid general paranoia of the *big brother*, father, mother-is-*watching* you variety. Much guilt is caused by feeling watched and measured by others. Most of the time those others really do not care! If they do, adopt a gentle "*So What*" attitude.

9. Assess your guilt by asking yourself if what you feel guilty about will cause some kind of permanent damage? Will it really matter in twenty years??

10. Lighten up on yourself. Give yourself the same soothing acceptance/forgiveness you might offer a friend who told you what he/she feels guilty about.

11. Force yourself *not* to feel guilty about feeling good about yourself.

12. Take more time out to care for yourself and forgive yourself.

Chapter 12

Increasing Your Self-Esteem Through Love

Viktor Frankl may have been the first person to phrase it in this manner that true self-esteem and a valid sense of identity can be found only in the reflected appraisal of those whom we have loved.

You can see, therefore, one of the easiest ways to increase your self-esteem is to love others, preferably in an unselfish, unconditional manner. The more you can love other people, the more you can increase your own feelings of self-worth.

Perhaps, one of the most valuable goals you could set for yourself to increase your self-esteem would be concerning love. Set a goal to love more people every day. A more specific goal would be to show more love to someone close to you that you have neglected. Or love someone around you who has a problem. Or show more kindness to employees or colleagues at work.

This chapter and this book are not primarily about love, but rather, about self-esteem. Yet, the concepts are almost synonymous. I must love (esteem) myself first before I can love you.

Jesus said it: "Love your neighbor as yourself." He meant you have to love yourself first, before you can love another person in the second instance.

Love and self-esteem, then, are completely interwoven. To increase your own self-esteem you must learn to love yourself more. And the best way to do that well is to practice loving others.

Self-Esteem Through Unconditional Love

Nothing else can enrich your human person, actualize your human growth potential, or bring you into the deepest meaning of life more than a love that is unconditional. Carl Rogers first really brought this to my awareness, and probably into the consciousness of most helping professionals by using the words "unconditional positive regard." Within its warming rays, any flower can grow.

Too many parents, bosses and even clergymen have been deluded for so long that criticisms, punishments and other corrective measures encourage

101

people to grow. They have never heard of the "Pygmalion Effect," evidenced so well in the life of Liza Doolittle of "My Fair Lady." It refers to the fact that if you expect people to do great and good things, they will do so. If you expect people to perform poorly, they will. The secret is lovingly to expect others to succeed. In the process, we will have more positive, realistic expectations of ourselves. Unconditional love is absolutely necessary for you to grow yourself or to aid others in their development.

Experiencing love to the fullest is necessary for you to have a meaningful life. Most people eventually come to the realization that their lives either already have meaning or must find some meaning. This is most obvious in the cases reported frequently in daily newspapers or popular magazines about suicides. At latest count, over 60,000 people deliberately kill themselves each year in the U.S.A. Those are only the ones reported directly as suicides, where it is all too obvious, like jumping off the Golden Gate Bridge.

Unfortunately, many thousands more each year commit suicide so that it looks like an accident. Those figures are not reported as suicides, for obvious reasons, such as to get insurance monies for the family, or to protect the living left behind.

Many suicide notes echo the same theme: "I have no reason to continue living."

All these people could not find love in their lives. Most of them just did not try hard enough. They surely did not try to implement the methods in this book which do work.

The sex therapists at SECS: Sexual Enrichment Counseling Services, Inc. in Chicago regularly report stories like this true one. Bill is a 62-year-old man, crying profusely, "I've never been to bed with a woman in my life, and it's killing me. I know I'm hopeless and I'm going to commit suicide." Bill's life was saved, first because a sex therapist loved him enough to take a risk and go all out to help him. Because Bill was so low in self-esteem, by ordinary therapy alone it could have taken months for him to build up sufficient self-esteem to invite a woman for a date.

But a SECS sexual surrogate therapist was also willing to take a risk for him, and lead him through a successful step-by-step program (reported elsewhere by Dean C. Dauw, Ph.D., in *The Stranger in Your Bed: A Guide to Emotional Intimacy*, Nelson-Hall, Inc., Chicago, 1979).

Bill was soon enabled to increase his self-esteem and find a woman to love him.

The power of love is unbelievable until you try it. You cannot appreciate how difficult it is to get some people even to try it. Disregard the Hitlers who may be paranoid schizophrenics and murder six million Jews. Disregard the Rev. James Jones-type messiahs who induce more than 900 hypnotized people into committing suicide in British Guyana. Disregard a John Wayne Gacy in Chicago who allegedly murdered 33 young men after having sex with them.

Consider, instead, how and why you must learn yourself to become more committed to another person and a cause of your choice. True love does not ask questions like "What am I getting out of this? Rather, your loving outreach to another person or cause will prove to you what Francis of Assisi said: "It is in giving that we receive."

Egoistic self-concern or egotistic self-concentration only lead to loss of self-esteem. That is the strange paradox you must learn.

You may observe in society a contemporary personalism. Its best insight may help you perceive that you become a person only if you receive your personhood from someone else, through the gift of affirmation. If you never experience yourself being valued by others, you will never value yourself. Affirm others to affirm yourself. That is the beauty of paying someone a sincere compliment. The sad fact is, people cannot readily accept compliments. They fear you are attempting to manipulate them. Thus, their unfounded fears lead to both parties losing. They lose a sincere gift of love. You may lose a chance to increase your own self-esteem by paying someone a sincere compliment.

In our society, we need to set up some kind of "Compliments Anonymous" organization, to teach everyone to give and receive sincere, valid compliments. Why should you wait until your mother is dead to put a rose on her grave? You can call up your mom today and give her a compliment. You can also do the same to anyone near you. Take time out right here and now to do it.

Viktor Frankl gave this absolutely true and necessary advice: "True self-esteem and a true sense of identity can be found only in the reflected appraisal of those whom we have loved."

Whenever you give the gift of love you receive far more than you give. It was probably the songwriter who first phrased it so well:

A bell isn't a bell 'till you ring it.
A song isn't a song 'till you sing it.
And love isn't love until you give it away.

When you give love, you realize the truest satisfaction in life. You will always live with the memory of having contributed to the lives of others.

A humorous sign in an office said it: "Have you hugged your boss lately?" Workplaces are some places where you spend most of your waking hours. Can you offer some more love or help to someone at work? It doesn't cost you any money, takes very little time and is returned to you in immeasurable ways.

Your increased self-esteem, satisfaction and fulfillment are the by-products of your dedicated love. Perhaps now is the best time for you to set a goal to show more love daily to someone at work, in your home or anywhere. **Now. Not tomorrow.**

You may be tempted to think that if you show or give love, you will receive instant rewards, and good times or fun. That is seldom the case. But it should not keep you from becoming more loving. You should not confuse loving with the expectation of immediate pleasure.

G. Marian Kinget writes On Being Human (Harcourt, Brace, Jovanovich, 1975):

103

Many a life may be regarded — and experienced by the subject — as good, yet, may comprise a relatively scant measure of what is commonly called fun and enjoyment. Among those who hold an examined view of the subject, few would deny that a fair share of the goodness of life befell to such persons as Abraham Lincoln, Ghandi, Louis Pasteur, Albert Schweitzer, Dorothea Dix, Dietrich Bonhoeffer, Pope John XXIII, Martin Buber, and Martin Luther King. Hardly anyone, however, would say that these persons' lives were marked by lots of fun. Such contamination of the notion of the good life with that of a good time obscures and distorts the issue.

Perhaps, then, you may become more aware that giving love does not necessarily result in immediate rewards. But it does result in eventually receiving greater self-esteem. Remember, however, that by setting a goal, then accomplishing it, you do get a more immediate payoff.

When you continue this process, each instant reward and payoff of achieving our goals eventually adds up to a greater level of self-esteem.

Ernie had to learn this the hard way. He was a handsome, young homosexual of 65 years. He cried as he said he had never lived with anyone, was lonely and did not believe he could find a man in gay society to live with for the rest of his life. He wanted me to help him become heterosexual because there were always nice women around whom he could find to love and live with.

One of his problems, perhaps his major problem, was a lack of true self-esteem from the very beginning of his life. When Ernie first came to SECS, his measured self-esteem was below zero. I explained to him the goal-setting method: one small step at a time. He was to begin by merely saying "hello" five times a day to any woman, anywhere. Mostly, his greetings were returned with smiles and a warmer hello. By continually setting small goals and reaping those instant rewards, Ernie was able to set riskier goals, one step at a time. Eventually, he did change his sexual orientation and achieve his long-range goal of finding more love.

Self-Esteem, Selfishness and Love

There is no pot of gold at the end of a rainbow. You do not really achieve happiness directly. It is, rather, a by-product of something else. For example, if you do good for someone else, such as a small helpless child, you may more readily experience joy and happiness. You simply cannot go to Sears and buy happiness directly. Self-fulfillment cannot be sought directly. It is, rather, a by-product of seeking something else. In my case, I can get some self-fulfillment by writing this book.

The human potential movement has been falsely criticized and is misunderstood by many in this regard. Critics have attacked Fritz Perls' great Gestalt Prayer as being too narcissistic.

> I do my thing and you do your thing.
> I am not in this world to live up to your expectations.
> And you are not in this world to live up to mine.

You are you and I am I.
If by chance we find each other, it's beautiful.
If not, it can't be helped.

One well-intentioned husband made this into a plaque for his wife as a Christmas present. She falsely interpreted it as meaning he intended to go out for an illicit love affair. It is so easy for people to misunderstand one another.

Fritz Perls was expressing the human need for self-expression and independence. I must treasure my very own feelings and thoughts. I must assert and exercise my healthy right to express them openly and freely. I can only make my own choices and you cannot make them for me. Fritz told me at an *Association for Humanistic Psychology* convention in 1967 in San Francisco that he wanted his words to counter the neurotically jealous possessiveness and clinging-vine dependency that hinder true love.

He did not really intend to wave the narcissistic subjectivism flag: "Do Your Own Thing Regardless of Others." That kind of subjectivism forgets we are interrelated, in a society of interdependent human beings.

If you are narcissistic, you ignore one of the most profound truths of human life. To be, for a person, means to be-with-others. Life, love, self-esteem, and fulfillment are all interrelated.

Perls' creed trumpets the human need for independence, but forgets the equally great, deepest human need for intensely loving relationships.

Perls' statement simply does not discuss all the warmth, caring, commitment and empathy that are essential to loving/giving/risking/sharing, to become a person of greater self-esteem.

Psychologist Walter Tubbs offers a supplement (*Journal of Humanistic Psychology*, 1972:12:5). It reflects a more complete view of life. True human fulfillment and greater self-esteem are found only in loving relationships: "The truth begins with two."

Beyond Perls

If I just do my thing and you do yours,
We stand in danger of losing each other
And ourselves.

I am not in this world to live up to your expectations.
But I am in this world to confirm you
As a unique human being
And to be confirmed by you.

We are fully ourselves only in relation to each other;
The I detached from a *Thou* disintegrates.
I do not find you by chance;
I find you by an active life
Of reaching out.

Rather than passively letting things happen to me,
I can act intentionally to make them happen.
I must begin with myself, true;
But I must not end with myself;
The truth begins with two.

Love: A Course In Miracles

The ideas and concepts of *A Course in Miracles* (Anonymous author. Tiburon: California, Foundation for Inner Peace; three volumes: text, manual and workbook) will be discussed in this and the remaining sections of this chapter. The effect and value of this course are truly unbelievable. If you sincerely study these volumes with an open mind, you will learn much more about yourself and love. Of particular interest is the contrast between "Thought System of the World" (the basics for teaching fear) and "Love's Thought System" (the basics for teaching only love).

World's Thought System

Very many people view the world as a snake pit filled with conflict, fear, confusion, chaos, anger, destruction, despair and war, with a hopeless future. They are convinced one madman pushing one button will end our small spaceship, planet Earth.

Naturally, many of us assert we want to live in a peaceful world at peace with ourselves. But how many truly believe this can occur? If we permit ourselves to accept the world's thought system, past will continue to predict future, and peace on earth will seem impossible. This system of thinking states that eventually we will be attacked, and if we wish to survive, we must defend ourselves better or attack first. According to the world's thought system, *fear is real* and the world is not loving and hostile.

These concepts spur us to give only in order to get and to put higher value on material assets, ranches, Porsches and trust funds. Success is based on what we own, rather than who we are.

In this world's thought system, we become preoccupied with the body's pleasures and pains. We foster insatiable physical desires. We can never be satisfied in a world that teaches us that our **self**/personality, not God, is in charge of our life. That leads us to believe happiness can only come from manipulating and controlling others.

Such a system also teaches us not to trust. It encourages us to keep ratings on people we like or dislike most. It causes us to teach our children nothing is consistent and that eventually we must have frustration, illness, depression, hopelessness and death.

In this pessimistic thought system, we are educated to believe that, if we analyze, interpret and make certain assumptions, we can learn how to judge and make decisions for continued happiness. But this never seems to occur. How can it, in a world where wars are perceived as normal? Where hurrying around, our minds suffused with scattered, random thoughts, is viewed as human nature.

The world's thought system wants us to believe there are good people and bad people, innocent and guilty; even some to be severely punished and executed for the good of the state. This world of insanity teaches us we must fight for peace, go to war for peace, devastate a Vietnamese village to save it; and view love as weakness. The world's thought system raises children to be seen and not heard, to "Do as I say, Not as I do!" Our example teaches children guilt and fear are real; life and body are the same; life as well as death is to be feared; and that it is normal to be ambiguous and ambivalent about everything in life.

The so-called experts, psychologists, ministers, judges and teachers have the same problems as others do in raising their children. (Cicero said the same thing in ancient Rome and Socrates, in ancient Greece). They seem to say we are either too permissive or too punitive in educating children and nothing seems to work.

Most of us continue to teach our children, despite the best intentions, fear, conflict and negative thinking as often as we teach love, peace and positive thinking. This is because according to the world's thought system, maturity means becoming more efficient and wiser at making judgements about other people, so that you can classify them. You can then more readily decide who is friend or foe.

Parents still inculcate guilt feelings in children to manipulate and change their behavior into acceptable forms. If children conform to the rules, we love them; if they don't, we withhold love and approval.

The world's thought system teaches love is conditional; receiving love depends on performance. Parents have measured and evaluated children and one another endlessly.

It may very well be that what we experience in the world is the result of the attitudes taught by our parents, ingested from our grandparents, which they unfortunately learned from their predecessors. Since we learn by what we teach, handing these attitudes on to our children, most of us live in a world where we feel little love.

If we continue in this unsuccessful manner, with its underlying hostilities, fears and lack of love, it is doubtful, if not impossible, we will ever have peace. Since the end of World War II, in 1946, we have suffered more than 126 major wars. The total keeps mounting. How much better it would be if, instead of educating our children, we could let them teach us.

Love's Thought System

Many people tend to believe a child's world is all "fantasy," while adults' world is all "real." We teach children that adults know more, are wiser than they, and that they must learn from us. Perhaps, just the opposite is true.

Suspend judgment momentarily as you read the following. Try to accept what may seem a different idea — that children can be our teachers and lead us out of our snake pit prison/bondage of fear which we accepted. Let us, through our children, recognize our purpose here on earth is to unite, to experience oneness by extending love and peace to others. Children teach us peace begins from within, not from without. Most of all, our children once again might teach us the meaning of **trust.**

To experience life differently requires letting go willingly of the belief that age determines who our teachers are. We need to cease believing that since adults have been around longer, we have more truths to teach children, than they do us.

A militant atheist friend once asked: "Was there ever a time when you felt the complete presence of love, the full presence of God?"

After reflection, this example occurred to me. Visiting new parents one day in a hospital, a light went on — a sense of wonder about the love this newborn child radiated to everyone. For a moment, I felt complete oneness with that innocent child, her mother, the nurse, the universe, everyone and everything in it. I was experiencing something thoroughly beyond any kind of intellectual understanding. At that moment I knew I was sharing complete love and the presence of God. The next day, back in class as a clinical psychology graduate student, analyzing and evaluating facts, love and the presence of God seemed to disappear.

More than ever before, I recognized the symbolic meaning of the newborn infant as teacher. Take a leap in faith now and look at the newborn infant in a different way, through a lens that sees only love.

Use your imagination to get inside the mind of a newborn infant. It is full of unconditional loving thoughts. The infant is unaware of her parents' body size or shape, what their life histories have been, what they say or think, or even if the parents are worthy of love. The child experiences the parents as perfectly joined with her in a love union, without separation.

The infant symbolizes knowledge, not as an aggregation of facts and statistics, but as love which is true knowledge. Love is the essence of her being, and the light she radiates can only be a reflection of God's love. Her spiritual being is real and everlasting and she innately knows her body is only a temporary outfit.

A newborn infant does not know death, and does not therefore fear death. She knows her true identity is love and that love never dies. In her "real world" there is only love. She does not understand past or future, experiencing this instant moment as the only time there is, an eternity to expand and extend love. Feeling completely loved by God, her only natural state is a union of love, joy and peace.

The newborn infant intuitively realizes you don't have a mind, — you **are** your mind, and all minds are joined. She does not experience separate minds or separation, but only oneness. She does not view herself as separate from anyone or anything else in the universe.

Knowing only one kind of love, her response to love is always total and complete, excluding no one. She cannot move even her little finger without moving her whole body/being. She does not confine her reality to her physical senses, to what she hears with her ears or sees with her eyes.

Appreciating her identity as love, she understands love asks no questions. **Love simply is.** She utters no words, but the highest form of love needs no words. She does not know jealousy or possessiveness, since she experiences complete union with all. She knows that as love, she is everything and everywhere. She knows love is complete absence of fear.

How much do parents interfere with the trust that an infant comes into the world symbolizing. Is not lack of trust one of the major problems of the world today? Is it not lack of trust that seems to be threatening the universe?

Small children express tremendous trust. If a 3 year old falls and hurts her knee, she runs to Mommy. Mommy kisses it and makes it better. Pain vanishes because the child experiences joining with her mother in a unity of love.

Can we permit the innocent newborn infant to become our mirror and teach us what we are — **love**? Can we permit the innocent infant in all of us to be awakened? Can we let go of the fearful child we have been fostering inside of us now and forever? Perhaps we can choose to see only the innocent loving child in everyone we meet, and let us know that whatever we see is only a reflection of ourselves.

Perhaps we can let a little child lead us into a world of oneness and union, into the only reality there is, a reality of never changing truth, a reality of love. Can we learn from the newborn infant to teach only love?

Three Basic Principles

Consider the basic ideas in *A Course in Miracles*. You have only two major emotions: love, your natural inheritance, and fear, which your mind has invented. In other words, instead of seeing others as attacking me, I may freely choose to alter my perception. I can see them as either loving, or fearful, which means giving a call of help for love. You will discover you can love a "fearful" person, but you may not be able to love someone perceived as attacking you.

These three basic ideas can bring you more peace of mind:

1. Set up your only major goal to have peace of mind, peace of God.
2. Make forgiveness your only function.
3. Do not make any decisions until you listen to your inner voice (which also goes by the gut sense, intuition, inner teacher or voice of God.)

When you begin to change your belief system to apply these principles to your life, positive, dramatic changes will occur. These fantastic changes will go far beyond an explanation that you are merely growing older and more accepting.

In changing our attitudes, the fundamental concept is that it is not people or conditions that cause us to be upset. Rather, it is our own thoughts and attitudes that need to be changed first. This concept, in complete opposition to the world's belief system, states that we are responsible for our feelings and experiences. We do not have to be **robots** who allow others to press our buttons and decide whether we will be happy or sad, at peace or conflict. We can take full responsibility for ourselves. By altering your attitudes and thoughts, you will change your perception of reality.

By letting go of negative, judgmental thoughts, you will have only loving ones. You will allow your mind to be completely free, full of love and peace and joined.

The world's belief system holds that everything in our external world is the cause, and we are the effects. Thus, when we are unhappy or in distress, we believe it is caused by someone or something in our external environment.

Whenever something goes wrong in our lives, when we are feeling a lack of love or having trouble with teaching love or being a loving parent, we are tempted by our past histories to feel like a victim. Then, we seek someone to blame. A part of our mind wants to blame our parents, the world or all those in it.

Forgiveness is the way to view the world differently. It is the key to letting go of the past, and to correcting our misperceptions. Forgiveness means letting go of whatever we think other people, the world or God have done to us, or whatever we think we did to them. Forgiveness is celestial amnesia. It is letting go of all memories of the past except the love we have given and received. Through forgiveness we can stop the endless recycling of guilt and view ourselves, our children, our parents, everyone else, including God, with love.

Children can teach us much about forgiveness. Consider, for example, two six year olds at play. Tommy comes running in to his mother, Rita, and says: "I am never going to play with Timmy again. He took my truck away." A few minutes later, she goes outside to find Tommy and Timmy perfectly happy. Tommy had let go of the event and had forgiven. Yet adults will often carry grudges and unforgiving thoughts for years. Whose reality is more correct? Whose reality is more peaceful?

In my role as management consultant at Human Resource Developers, Inc., I was called out to a client company. Along came thirteen year old Annie, a victim of cancer. At the meeting, one of the divisional executives was very angry because a competitor had hired away a valuable employee who was going to be hard to replace.

Annie spontaneously rose to the occasion, asked the executive if he was upset, and he naturally said "yes." Then Annie asked: "If you could be any-where in the world where you would be relaxed and peaceful, where would it be?" His answer was "Waikiki, Hawaii." Annie suggested he close his eyes and imagine he was in Hawaii feeling relaxed, joined as one with the warm sand, cool Pacific and azure sky. Annie continued: "You know, Mister, you can't be relaxed or feel peaceful as long as you are angry. You won't be able to make good decisions until you forgive your competitor and the guy he stole away. Forgiveness is just letting go, letting the event just float away."

Later, the divisional executive said: "You know, if you had told me the same thing, I might not have been open to it. But your 13 year old Annie got through to me. She made it seem very clear and simple." Children have a way of being right on.

Many of us live in a world of anguish, wondering where the next attack will come from. How can we eliminate these fearful attack thoughts? It is easier than we think, if we will let go of the old belief system. Forgiveness is the way. It removes road-blocks to the awareness of love's presence. it allows the

110

miracle of love to occur. Forgiveness enables us to heal all our relationships so there is no separation.

We cannot really experience or teach love until all blame for everything and anything has disappeared. We cannot be truly loving to our children, ourselves and others while still blaming someone else or ourselves. We cannot show total love to our children until we have healed all our relationships. Forgiveness is the key to happiness because it removes all hurdles to love. Forgiveness can enable us to live in a world of all-inclusive love.

' One major method to accomplish these steps is to achieve control over all our undisciplined thoughts. We need to see the value in quieting our minds, while believing in fact we can do it. Begin with a few minutes every day. Gradually increase your silent time. It is not crucial whether you call it meditation, prayer or simply quieting the mind. What **is** important is to go toward peace. As you quiet your mind and yourself, you'll be able to hear that inner voice tell you what to do.

The following ten steps can help you remember the innocent child in all of us. Consider these ten steps as a path toward peace that, when actualized, can transform the world into a place where consistent love and peace will be pervasive.

Paths to Peace

1. Forgive your parents totally.
2. Forgive everyone who has ever been here, who is here now, or who will ever be here, including ourselves, **totally.**
3. Forgive the world, totally.
4. Forgive God totally.
5. Make a leap in faith and trust in love, trust in God.
6. Choose to experience peace rather than conflict.
7. Choose to experience love rather than fear.
8. Choose to be a love finder rather than a fault finder.
9. Choose to be a love giver rather than a love seeker.
10. Teach only love.

World's Thought System
Teaching Fear

1. Reality is limited to your body. It is impossible to live in this world without fear, depression, conflict and worry.

2. We experience ourselves as fearful when we try to get as much as we can, hold onto it and view ourselves as separate from others.

3. Age and experience determine who our teachers are.

4. Love is always conditional; I will love you if you perform and behave as I want you to.

Love's Thought System
Teaching Love

1. Our natural state of being is love. It is to be joyful, happy, peaceful.

2. We experience ourselves as love only when we are constantly giving our love and peace away and are joining others as one.

3. Everyone is our teacher of love, regardless of age.

4. Love is always **unconditional,** and has nothing to do with behavior or performance.

5. There are different kinds of love; a love for this and that; there are different degrees of love. And there are people who should be excluded from love because their behavior has made them unworthy of love.

6. This moment is for fear. Fearful past predicts fearful present and future. Spend most of your time worrying about past and future. Don't let yourself experience joy now.

7. Body, life and love all die. Life and body are same. Life and love are separate.

8. Love is limited to what we see and hear. It has boundaries and expectations.

9. Everything we see is separate and different from what we are.

10. What is true is that we are born to live in a world where sooner or later we will experience pain, unhappiness, despair, fear, hopelessness and death. There are a lot of things besides love in this world.

5. There is **only love,** and it is always total and maximal and excludes no one.

6. This instant is for love and it is the only instant there is.

7. Life is separate from the body. Life and love are one and the same: Life is always, because love never dies.

8. Love has **no** limits, boundaries or expectations. It unfolds simply upon itself.

9. Everything we see only mirrors who we are.

10. What is true can only be love and what is love is all that there is.

Chapter 13

Developing a Sound Self-Esteem Lifestyle

"Dumbo" in Walt Disney's movie of the same name is an excellent example of what this book is all about. You will remember Dumbo as a little, young elephant with very huge ears. When Dumbo was asleep, he could actually fly by flapping his ears like a bird's wings. But alas, when Dumbo was awake, he could only walk like other elephants. His bird friends could not persuade him that he was that unexpected creature, the flying elephant.

With a flash of insight, one of his bird friends plucked an ordinary feather from his own tail. He presented it to Dumbo in a fascinating story about the magic feather. It was supposed to enable its bearer to fly. To give credence to the story, the birds told Dumbo the magic feather was the method used by mother birds to teach their children how to fly.

Dumbo accepted the gift and attributed "flying-inducing power" to the feather. Clutching the magic feather in his trunk, he was able to soar. Eventually, he lost the feather and was unable to fly at will when awake.

Then, finally, Dumbo's friends were able to convince him the feather was really not magical and he could finally fly by himself.

Dumbo represents an interesting example of what this book is asking you to consider. In his initial state, Dumbo possessed the ability to fly but he was unable to attribute that talent to himself. Hence, he could not fly. When Dumbo received the feather and misattributed the flying power to its magic rather than his own unexpected capabilities, he flew very well. Later, when Dumbo was actually confronted with all the facts that he had been soaring and that his attribution of the cause to the feather was incorrect, he was really able to attribute correctly the ability to himself. Dumbo could then fly without external aid.

The intervening misattribution fulfilled a persuasive role that was impossible merely with the first evidence available to his senses and to his nose (so to speak). Dumbo, of course, is just a story. Yet, if attribution theory can persuade a cartoon elephant that he can soar merely by flapping his ears, imagine its power when you apply this process to yourself.

113

There is a little bit of Dumbo in all of us. Psychologists have shown that the attribution of events and causes results in determining, modifying or altering how you feel about yourself.

To develop the level of self-esteem that you really want, you need to learn better how to attribute the correct abilities to yourself. You must stop "selling yourself short."

One helpful way to accomplish this method is by attributing self-confidence to your real personality. Do not be phoney. Just be yourself "in a confident way." In other words, you need to role play yourself being confident. Just try to imagine yourself as the self-confident person you want to be. Then do it.

Just like Dumbo, you need to stop looking for a magic feather. You need to give yourself credit for the hidden abilities you already have. They need to be brought out of the closet — out of a state of mere possibility to a state of real actuality. It is just as easy to give yourself the self-esteem you desire, as it was to talk yourself out of it in the first place.

Dumbo talked himself out of flying. The birds talked him into it.

In the same way you need to convince yourself right here and now that you can talk your way into it. You can fly higher on the magical wings of greater self-esteem.

When you begin to change your belief system or philosophy, you change not just one feeling, but rather an entire spectrum of feelings and behaviors.

Consider what is the most important **false belief** or irrational idea you may now be holding about yourself. Some friend or relative will know, if you don't. As comics always say: "Behind every successful man, there is always a wife telling him he's not so hot."

Even if you do not have a helpful spouse or partner, you may have a boss or colleague at work who can give you some enlightening feedback. All you need is the openness to ask.

Consider how few people are willing to be open and ask for feedback. Some are willing to ask but unable to accept the results of the feedback.

Developing a sound self-esteem lifestyle means you may have to cease conforming. That was one message of a previous chapter about learning to become a bigger risk-taker. Human beings seem to have developed an irrational need to **overconform**. Great philosophers and psychologists like Albert Ellis have increasingly emphasized the only way you can be truly liberated is to be highly disapproved of by much of the people, much of the time. (If you want to understand his theories more clearly, investigate all of Ellis' research on rational-emotive-therapy: RET.)

In modern times, Albert Ellis was first to emphasize you feel as you think. If you think you are a "Dumbo-dumbshit," you feel "dumb-shitty," or at least "shitty."

You need to keep asking yourself what you **really** desire in life and keep experimenting and trying. You need to take some reasonable risks to discover if what you think you want is what you **really** do want.

In that process, however, you must not fool yourself that anything or everything you want, from yourself or others, **must, should** or **ought** to exist.

114

You may not need, for example, a daily orgasm, or multiple orgasms, or 100 million dollars. But you can reasonably desire and expect a valid level of self-esteem, or sufficient aid from friends and lovers to increase your self-esteem.

Ellis is especially correct when he emphasizes "**shouldhood** equals shithood." That's one reason you may have a level of self-esteem that is lower than you deserve. From the time we were little kids our parents, schools, churches, and society have all been brainwashing us with too many "**shoulds**."

. In the language of transactional analysis, we have too many overconforming parent tapes in our heads. "**You must do this.**" or "**You should not do that**."

Ellis phrased it in an incomparable fashion: "We have too much **musterbation**." "Shouldhood equals shithood." You need to learn to make everything you do "**nonsacred**." For example, if you make sexual behavior so overly sacred, you develop a "Madonna complex." This is a very common sexual hangup among men with mostly religious backgrounds. They have been "**should-ed**" into believing: "Save your love for your wife; sex is only for prostitutes." As a result, then, too many men deprive not only their wives of more love, but also may more easily become impotent, bored, divorced, or all the above.

You need to dispute more of your beliefs, as a way to develop a higher self-esteem lifestyle.

Consider the following method of learning how to change negatives to positives. During the next 24 hours, resolve to speak hopefully about everything: your health, your career, your whole future life. Make an effort to speak optimistically about everything. This may be difficult at first because you may have fallen into the Dumbo-like habit of thinking unsuccessfully or pessimistically. You need to unlearn the old bad habit and substitute a new, good habit pattern.

After thinking and talking optimistically for 24 hours, you will become convinced you can do it more for one whole week. Then you could take a break and be more "realistic" for just one or two days. You will see that what you considered to be "realistic" a week ago was actually pessimistic; but what you now view as "realistic" is something entirely unique: the awareness of your new positive view of life. Remember that when most of your acquaintances say they are being realistic, they delude themselves: they are really being **negative.**

If you are a religious believer, start at the beginning of the New Testament and underline every sentence about **faith**. Continue until you have highlighted every passage in all four books of Matthew, Mark, Luke and John. Study Mark 11, verses 22, 23, and 24. These ideas will be good examples of concepts to fix deeply in your consciousness.

Memorize these verses. Try to remember one each day until you can playback the complete list from your memory. This may require a little time and effort, but remember you have invested much more time becoming a

115

negative thinker than this will require. You will need a little more effort and energy to unlearn your bad, negative habit.

Discover the most positive thinkers among your friends. Then, definitely try to spend more time with them. You need not cast aside your negative friends but cultivate your positive peers for a while, until you can learn to imitate their outlook. You will be able to return later to your negative friends to present them a more hopeful viewpoint.

You can practice countering anyone's pessimistic statements with more positive, optimistic attitudes. You need not necessarily make yourself an argumentative bore, but rather someone attempting to uplift a friend's spirits.

The American historian, Charles Beard, was giving his final lecture at Columbia University. A young student asked him to sum up what was the most important thing he had learned in a lifetime. Beard replied: "When it is dark enough, you can see the stars."

Perhaps you, too, can learn better to understand that, regardless of how dark or how your self-esteem has been in the past, you can begin to see the stars.

The reverence of a man's self is, next to religion, the chiefest bridle of all vices.
— Lord Bacon

Chapter 14

Self-Esteem and Self-Actualization

Jesse Jackson said: "You may not be responsible for being down, but you are responsible for getting up."

Jerry was fired from his $100,000.00-a-year job as a vice-president in a manufacturing company. He felt extremely depressed. His anxiety was so high it broke all thermometers. He was freaking his wife out with all his crazy actions, whenever he was not merely slumped down watching the soaps on TV.

The company that fired him had no desire to aid the managers who had been ground up and spat out. So, Jerry was not sent to a professional outplacement firm for recycling. Fortunately, Jerry's brother knew of one. He sent his disconsolate relative to Human Resource Developers.

The HRD psychologist listened carefully as Jerry unraveled his tale of grief.

"I always doubted my self-worth. I seemed to be looking back over my shoulder all the time. The pressures always seemed to be getting to me much more easily than the other group. I felt my grip slipping on all the projects. I guess I never **really** developed any real self-confidence."

Jerry's level of self-esteem was very low throughout his whole life. He had never developed a good healthy way of valuing himself and his talents. And he did not know how to go about doing it.

The distinguished psychologist, Abraham Maslow, pointed out the fact that Jerry, as well as every other executive, or housewife or student has a basic hierarchy of needs. In reality, they are stages of personal growth. You must satisfy the first level of need before you can hope to attain the next highest. It's very much like climbing a ladder.

The lowest level of need is for food, clothing and shelter. Once you have enough of these, you may be able to satisfy your safety needs. Everyone wants protection against danger, deprivation, insecurity. We want a predictable environment.

The third highest level is to seek satisfaction for our social needs. You want to belong, to have friends, and to be accepted. You want to give and receive attention, to love and be loved.

Once you have attained a measure of your social needs, you are in a much better position to achieve your ego needs, the fourth level. This is where self-esteem comes in. You want to feel competent in your career. You need and

117

deserve strong feelings of self-confidence, independence, achievement, mastery, recognition, appreciation, respect.

Most people, unfortunately, never achieve that level, to any strong degree, if at all. They can become fixated, perhaps, at some lower level. They never achieve enough positive feelings about themselves. That is one reason why this book is written: To help you achieve a valid level of self-esteem.

Then, you will finally be enabled to move on to the highest level — self-actualization.

You will eventually want to realize your true potential. You want to exercise your creativity. You want to develop all your talents and project your own ideas.

The level of self-actualization is an ideal for all to strive toward. Few people, however, reach it, because they do not first attain their level of self-esteem.

You are now the realization of your greatest potential. So far, that is.

You will want more, however. The reason is because the need to self-actualize is within each of us. Your motive toward self-actualizing is innate. Each of us has an inherent need to be for the sake of being, to do for the sake of doing, to feel for the sake of feeling, to be self-actualizing.

According to Maslow, a self-actualizing person is not a super-person, but a fulfilling one. If you are self-actualizing, you have the following character-istics.

(1) Effective perception: you see the world and yourself as they really are. You are never phony, but congruent. You don't, for example, have such a low level of self-esteem that you must put on a show to cover it up.

(2) Honesty to be who you really are: you want to feel and express your true feelings and thoughts.

(3) You want to seek out your feelings rather than avoid them.

Now that you have a clearer idea of self-actualization, the goal you want to achieve, you can perhaps be more motivated to develop your self-esteem.

The assumption here is simple: you will want to become more self-actualized. Therefore, you will want to develop your self-esteem so you can get there.

In achieving a sufficient level of self-esteem, you also need to consider esteem from others. One way to get that is to set goals to achieve your potentials. By developing your talents, you will be able to make contributions, however-large or small, and as a result attain a level of significance and relevance. By recognizing your relevance, you will obtain feelings of self-pride and self-respect. Others will recognize and appreciate your contributions. Your self-esteem will increase.

Psychologist Everett Shostrom, in his "Dimensions of Being," suggests that you develop your esteem through sequential steps: being adequate, capable, worthwhile, important and "being your power."

Beginning with the state of being adequate, you are merely accepting yourself as you really are, while acknowledging your limitations. You need not be a "super-person." It is far more important to be **you.**

In the challenge of realizing your potentials, you may experience the frustration of wanting to know something, but not want to expend the effort of learning. "I want to play the piano, but I don't think I'll ever get those damned chords." That feeling of frustration comes from comparing yourself with others who have already grown to realize their potentials, or from falsely anticipating how long it will take you to realize such proficiency. Your frustration can be lessened by not falsely comparing (*You* **are** *unique*), and by not anticipating (**experience now**).

You are at the beginning. Experience the growth process and your emotional involvement with it. Dwell on the joy of today's progress and achievement. Non-self actualizing people typically consider it difficult to be merely adequate and refuse to recognize their limitations. They bluff their way through life as did Jerry described in the beginning of this chapter. Such people pretend too much. They may have only little knowledge about a particular subject, but attempt to pawn themselves off as "experts unlimited." Most of the energy that could be devoted to personal growth will be diverted into preserving the deception.

As you increasingly enhance your skills, you will gain more self-confidence. Then you will be able to experience the spontaneity and freedom associated with becoming **capable.** Being capable assures you that most challenges are well within the limitations of your talents. You will have attained a definite level of expertise. Some of your friends may find great personal satisfaction and pride in being capable, and stop growing at this level. For some, growth will progress to a state of feeling **worthwhile.**

Being worthwhile means you are adding something of yourself to whatever you are involved in. Your personal signature is added to your contributions. Your own panache distinguishes your contributions from others. Your uniqueness becomes more obvious. Your individual style permits your contributions to be identified as coming **only** from you. You are unique in the whole universe. Irreplaceably so. By being worthwhile, you recognize what you do, say, think or feel is very worthwhile.

You need to attain a sense of being worthwhile regardless of others' evaluations. Your value is still there even though others may not appreciate you and your contributions. Others will be unable to come close to your style and so they cannot recognize your talents. By being unable to duplicate your style, others will learn to appreciate your skills. That song really says it. I've often felt that way but could never find the words: "Love isn't love until you give it away..."

The fourth level of self-esteem is feeling "important." You need to develop beyond the stage of feeling worthwhile to being important. You will believe you are as important as anyone else. You become not necessarily "rich" nor "famous" but **somebody.**

You develop a sense of honor, pride and dignity in being who you are. You are as valuable, and important as anyone else. Your caring has merit. If you lack feelings of importance, you may consign yourself to a lower slot when compared with others, believing their needs, desires and feelings are more important than yours. Such faulty ideas lead you into too much self-sacrifice.

Attitudes of putting yourself down lead to self-contempt. "Here, you take my place. I'm a born loser." After you finally believe you are important, then your attitude adds to your lifestyle of sincere caring, giving and pride. Once you enhance your feelings of being important, you can begin to experience your **sense of power**.

By experiencing your sense of power, you can abandon yourself to really living fully. You can take the risk of being yourself. You can cope more effectively. You will no longer need to seek excuses for not throwing yourself into the zest and joy of living. You may lose the prestige of a job, but it will not threaten your feelings of importance. You may lose a love, but not be devastated. With your feelings of power will come a sense of freedom. Freedom to experience life to its fullest degree.

Some people seem to have a sense of their own power. But they misuse it. Non-self-actualizing people may view this power falsely as the chance to get whatever they want, regardless of the outcome, or exploit whomever they wish despite the agony. Many executives and managers do this daily wherever you work. Sometimes, the only way in which they can learn to experience their own weakness is when they are fired themselves.

In fact, the best definition of a "peak experience" is when you can experience your power and weakness at the same time. When you are weak, you can still feel worthwhile and important. You can share more than one state of being simultaneously. You can feel worthwhile and vulnerable at the same time, or important and secure at the same time. The difference is clear: a person striving toward a valid level of self-esteem can be aware of the differences and accept them.

People with low self-esteem, on the other hand, have to hide or deny their awareness of the differences.

After you increase your level of self-esteem, you can begin to strive toward self-actualization. This is the great goal you can achieve.

How to Become More Self-Actualized

The self-actualized person has been called by many names, since he was first clearly described by Abe Maslow. Carl Rogers wrote about the "fully-functioning person"; Marie Jahoda, the "mentally healthy"; Sidney Jourard, the "disclosed self"; Charles Morris, the "open self"; and Ted Landsman, "the beautiful and noble person".

At the same time, there has been much research on truly creative people by men like Don MacKinnon, Calvin Taylor and E. Paul Torrance.

Regardless of whose system or what adjectives, self-actualized people are surely those people who have risen to their full stature emotionally. They are truly in touch with their own feelings and are therefore better enabled to understand and accept the feelings of others. Because they are more in touch with reality, they are able to be more perceptive and accepting of themselves and the world. They can be unconventional and spontaneous without calling too much attention to the differences.

Individuals so "centered" receive much satisfaction from inside themselves, enabling them to appreciate solitude more than other people do.

Although they are typically able to get along well with others, they do not really need them and are self-directed. They may be typically free of the need to impress others or be liked by them.

Because self-actualized people have a great ability to love, they are very open, spontaneous and giving in their love relationships. As creative people, they are divergent in their thought processes rather than convergent or constricted. Experiencing a deep empathy, they can enjoy profound relationships with others.

Perhaps one of their most endearing traits is their continuing wonder with life — being able to enjoy almost ecstatically each new rainbow, sunrise or sunset.

Although the above description is not perfect, (you would have to paraphrase all the above mentioned authors for the most complete picture), it does give some idea of individuals.

How can people become more self-actualized? Maslow suggested at least eight ways you can begin, and briefly paraphrased here:

(1) Make a great effort to experience totally each and every single moment. Try to get "into" it as unselfconsciously as a young child, becoming fully absorbed in it to the exclusion of all else. You may occasionally be having such intense moments now. But you can make them happen more often and prolong them. "At this moment of experiencing," said Maslow, "the person is wholly and fully human...This is a moment when the self is actualizing itself."

This especially means living in the here and now. It is surprising how many people are usually re-living the past or worrying about the future. They forget we make our future out of fully functioning **here and now**.

(2) View life as a "process of choices, one after another." Everyone has to make myriads of choices daily. Each time you are actually deciding to progress or regress; to really be developing and growing or falling back on habits or fears. Try to make more and more growth choices. According to Maslow, "self-actualization is an ongoing process." By making a growth choice instead of a fear choice dozens of times daily, you can "move a dozen times a day toward self-actualization."

(3) Really listen to the "impulse voices" within yourself. Look inside yourself for your own decisions, tastes and interests. Maslow explained: "Most of us listen not to ourselves but to Mommy's introjected voice or Daddy's voice or to the voice of the Establishment, or of the elders, of authority or of tradition." It's actually more healthy to concentrate on how you yourself really feel about something, not on how you think you are expected to feel.

(4) "When in doubt, be honest rather than not." Most people are really full-fledged game players. (See E. Berne's *Games People Play* and T. Harris' *I'm Okay, You're Okay*.) Or they seek discretion and diplomacy rather than honesty and openness.

121

A truly honest person, however, will be looking to himself for answers and will be taking responsibility for whatever he finds in himself. And each time you take responsibility for yourself, you are taking a greater step toward actualizing yourself.

(5) Be a courageous risk-taker. Dare to be unique. Risk making even a seemingly unpopular statement if that is how you really feel. Maslow noted that even in the so-called avant-garde art world, a conformity of taste is demanded. Many people try too hard to make sophisticated pronouncements about something they really may not understand or even like. A self-actualized person may admit "that puzzles me. I'll have to think about it." A person who is willing to take the risk can more often than not succeed because it becomes a positive, self-fulfilling prophecy. It's surprising how a risk-taker can be more successful than someone considered a dishonest phony.

(6) Discover what you **really, really** want to do, and work hard to do it very well. Become as outstanding as you really can. This may mean, of course, going through an arduous period of education or self-preparation. Executive consultants have found, by researching their clients in a management consulting firm, that there are large numbers of top executives and men on the way up seeking some career guidance as a means of becoming more self-actualized.

(7) Open yourself up to peak experiences — "little moments of ecstasy" — for they are fleeting glimpses of self-actualization. Try to set up conditions in which peak experiences may be most likely to happen, and treasure them when they do occur, as in number one above. Maslow became convinced almost everyone had a few peak experiences, but "some people wave these small mystical experiences aside" and deny them.

(8) Try to identify your defenses. (This relates to #4 and 5 above, too.) These are self-defeating behavior patterns you have developed over the years, mostly as a result of our total previous environment and because of not following the seven previous routes to self-actualization. Although it may be painful, it surely is necessary — repressing or suppressing a problem won't solve it.

If you can make the daily efforts to follow these suggestions, — especially toward finding out who you really are, what you really like, what you can become — then you are on the road to self-actualization.

Appendices

Barksdale Self-Esteem Index No. 69*

SE can be measure and studied in many ways.

The methods and ideas used in this book are the results of many years of research. In the future, we will be continuing to develop more creative techniques.

Some of the most innovative methods and instruments have already been developed by L.S. "Barks" Barksdale. He has given permission to reprint the following Barksdale SE index No. 69 and the Barksdale Life Style Evaluation No. 70a.

Self-Esteem is an emotion. It is how warm and loving you feel toward yourself, based on your sense of self-worth and importance. **No one** raised in our value judging culture can escape a significant lack of Self-Esteem. A low score on this evaluation is, thus, no reflection on you as a person and nothing to be ashamed or embarrassed about. Your existing level of Self-Esteem simply is what it **is** — the product of faulty cultural conditioning. No matter how low your present Self-Esteem Index (SEI) may be, you can raise it to any desired level by working with The Barksdale Foundation Self-Esteem Program.

This Self-Esteem Index measures your current level of Self-Esteem and serves as a gauge of your progress in achieving **sound** Self-Esteem. It is important to **you** to clearly understand all statements and be completely honest in your scoring if you are to obtain a valid Index. It is also essential that you answer these statements according to how you actually **feel** or **behave,** rather than how you **think** you "**should**" feel or behave.

Score as follows (each score shows how true **or** the amount of time you believe that statement is true for **you**):

> 0 = not at all true for me
> 1 = somewhat true **or** true only part of the time
> 2 = fairly true **or** true about half of the time
> 3 = mainly true **or** true most of the time
> 4 = true all the time

*© 1974 by Lilburn S. Barksdale, The Barksdale Foundation, P.O. Box 187, Idyllwild, California 92349.

(This is an **evaluation**, not a test.)

Score   **Self-Esteem Statements**

_____ 1. I don't feel anyone else is better than I am.

_____ 2. I am free of shame, blame and guilt.

_____ 3. I am a happy, carefree person.

_____ 4. I have no need to _prove_ I am as good as or better than others.

_____ 5. I _do not_ have a strong need for people to pay attention to me or like what I do.

_____ 6. Losing _does not_ upset me or make me feel "less than" others.

_____ 7. I feel warm and friendly toward myself.

_____ 8. I _do not_ feel others are better than I am because they can do things better, have more money, or are more popular.

_____ 9. I am at ease with strangers and make friends easily.

_____ 10. I speak up for my own ideas, likes and dislikes.

_____ 11. I am not hurt by others' opinions or attitudes.

_____ 12. I _do not_ need praise to feel good about myself.

_____ 13. I feel good about others' good luck and winning.

_____ 14. I _do not_ find fault with my family, friends or others.

_____ 15. I _do not_ feel I must always please others.

_____ 16. I am open and honest and not afraid of letting people see my real self.

_____ 17. I am friendly, thoughtful and generous towards others.

_____ 18. I do not blame others for _my_ problems and mistakes.

_____ 19. I enjoy being alone with myself.

_____ 20. I accept compliments and gifts without feeling uncomfortable or needing to give something in return.

_____ 21. I admit my mistakes and defeats without feeling ashamed or "less than."

_____ 22. I feel no need to defend what I think, say or do.

126

_____ 23. I *do not* need others to agree with me or tell me I'm right.

_____ 24. I *do not* brag about myself, what I have done, or what my family has or does.

_____ 25. I *do not* feel "put down" when criticized by my friends or others.

_____ **Self-Esteem Index** (sum of all scores)

Name _____ Date_____

To find your self-esteem index (SEI), simply add scores of all Self-Esteem Statements. The possible range of your Self-Esteem Index is from 0 to 100. Sound Self-Esteem is indicated by an SEI of 95 or more. Experiences shows that any score under 90 is a disadvantage, a score of 75 or less is a serious disadvantage, and an SEI of 50 or less indicates a really crippling lack of Self-Esteem.

Barksdale Life Style Evaluation No. 70a

(This is an **evaluation**, not a test.)

The following statements describe a life style that is in alignment with reality and essential to achieving and maintaining **sound** Self-Esteem. This *evaluation* is an index of your current Life Style and a beginning reference point in your progress toward developing a Life Style that generates and maintains Sound Self-Esteem. Careful inspection of these statements discloses their vital importance to functioning in a harmonious and constructive manner. Make every effort to comply with them, if you want to achieve Sound Self-Esteem. Do not, however, feel "less than," ashamed or guilty if you are not doing as well as you feel you "should." Simply realize that you are **always** doing the **best** your prevailing Awareness and current Self-Esteem permit.

Score as follows (each score shows how true **or** the amount of time you believe that statement is true for **you**):

> 0 = not at all true for me
> 1 = somewhat true **or** true only part of the time
> 2 = fairly true **or** true about half the time
> 3 = mainly true **or** true most of the time
> 4 = true all the time

Score	Life Style Statements
_____	1. I accept complete responsibility for my own well-being — for everything I think, say, do and *feel*.
_____	2. I am my own authority for everything I do and direct my life in constructive channels.
_____	3. I make decisions promptly and willingly accept the consequences.
_____	4. I discipline myself through monitoring my thoughts, desires, images and expectations.

_____ 5. I think for myself and act accordingly.

_____ 6. I allow myself the freedom to make mistakes, to be "wrong," to fail, free of self-accusation, guilt or feeling "less than."

_____ 7. I take deep satisfaction in doing my work conscientiously and well.

_____ 8. I approach every problem and new endeavor with confidence.

_____ 9. I do not blame others for my problems, mistakes, defeats or handicaps.

_____ 10. I do not procrastinate or drift; I motivate myself in line with my chosen life objectives.

_____ 11. I follow all undertakings through to a logical conclusion.

_____ 12. I do not allow personal comparisons to affect my sense of worth.

_____ 13. I do not try to prove my worth by my accomplishments.

_____ 14. I defer to no one on account of his wealth or status.

_____ 15. I do not blame myself for my mistakes, defeats or failures.

_____ 16. I stand up for my own values, opinions and convictions.

_____ 17. I refrain from no endeavor because of fear of failure or defeat.

_____ 18. I do not require others' confirmation or agreement and approval to do as I, myself, see fit.

_____ 19. I do not let others talk me into things against my better judgment.

_____ 20. I am patient, kind and gentle with myself.

_____ 21. I take the initiative in personal contacts and relationships.

_____ 22. I walk erect and face everyone with a friendly countenance.

_____ 23. I do not deny my needs, feelings or opinions to please others.

_____ 24. I am frank and open with everyone, free of all masks and pretentions.

_____ 25. I do not try to impress others with my worth or importance.

_____ **Life Style Index** or "LSI" (sum of scores for all statements)

Name _____ Date_____

To find your life style index (LSI), simply add scores of all Life Style Statements. The possible range of your Life Style Index is from 0 to 100.

Exercise for Increasing Self-Esteem

Inventory of Strengths

Most people really are not aware of or appreciate all the good qualities, traits or abilities that they already possess.

Consider this example. Graduate students working on their MBA degree at night while working as executives and managers during the day were asked to do a simple thing. They were told to imagine an employer wanted to know all their good abilities to decide about hiring them. Can you guess what was the average number of good talents, abilities or assets they wrote? Three! Only three!

Before you read on, you may want to try that same sample exercise. Write down somewhere in this book all your good qualities, abilities and the like. Date it, so that later on, you can reward yourself by seeing how much progress you have made since that time.

Then, look at the following list of categories. You should be able to detail certain assets in each category. Anything that you have done well in the past which still interests you or which you still enjoy doing represents a strength. You can list more than you may suspect at this very moment.

Try hard.

After you have finished, continue to repeat those qualities to yourself daily. As you become more aware of your strengths, you will begin to believe them, and act in a more confident manner. Your self-esteem will increase, and you will feel better about yourself.

Inventory of Strengths

Instructions:

To make an inventory of your strengths and resources, write each of the following headings, which indicate various areas of strength, on a separate sheet of paper and list under each heading your assets in that area. Anything that you have done well in the past which you still enjoy doing represents a strength and should be listed.

Sports and Outdoor Activities

Hobbies and Crafts

Expressive Arts

Health

Education, Training, and Related Areas

Work, Vocation, Job or Position

Special Aptitudes or Resources

Strengths through Family and Others

Intellectual Strengths

Aesthetic Strengths

Organizational Strengths

Imaginative and Creative Strengths

Relationship Strengths

Spiritual Strengths

Emotional Strengths

Other Strengths:

Humor

Liking to adventure or pioneer

Ability to stick your neck out

Perseverance or stick-to-it-iveness

Ability to manage finances

Knowledge of languages or cultures

Ability to speak in public

Making the best of your appearance

About the Author

Dean C. Dauw (pronounced Dow), Ph.D., is a licensed, registered clinical psychologist in private practice in Chicago. He is one of a few Chicago sex therapists certified by the American Association of Sex Educators, Counselors, and Therapists (AASECT). He is director of clinical services for Sexual Enrichment Counseling Services, Inc., a private sex therapy clinic located at 112 West Oak Street in Chicago (312-644-1920.)

Dr. Dauw is an associate professor in the DePaul University Graduate School of Business in Chicago, where he currently teaches courses in interpersonal relationships and communications. He is the author of seven books, including *The Stranger in Your Bed: A Guide to Emotional Intimacy* (Nelson-Hall, 1979), and *Increasing Your Self-Esteem: How to Feel Better About Yourself* (Waveland, 1980), and over 100 professional papers and articles. Three additional books, two concerning relationships and marriage games, will be published in 1984-85.

Dr. Dauw also is the principal author of two audiocassette self-help programs: *Intimacy—the Key to Building a Special Relationship* (1981), and *Self-Esteem and Risk Taking for Success* (1982), both produced by Human Resource Developers, Chicago.

Dr. Dauw received his doctorate in clinical psychology from the University of Minnesota. He is an active member of the American Psychological Association, past president of the Industrial Psychologists Association, and a frequent guest on Chicago-area and nationally syndicated radio and television programs.

The Stranger in Your Bed is the first and only book to be written by a psychologist on the use of sexual surrogates in treating sexual dysfunction problems. *Sex Therapy Innovations* is also the first and only book to include original research on surrogate-assisted sex therapy (Chapter 7).

While the use of surrogates is controversial within the field, and while its effectiveness as a therapeutic approach is often questioned, Dr. Dauw points out that the approach was pioneered by Masters and Johnson and that research indicates the success rate in treating such sexual dysfunctions as impotence and premature ejaculation through a closely supervised program of psychotherapy and surrogate assistance is substantially higher than reported success rates from conventional programs.

135

Comments Anyone?

We would appreciate your feedback. Please write or call:

Dean C. Dauw, Ph.D.
Sexual Enrichment Counseling Services, Inc.
112 West Oak Street
Chicago, Illinois 60610
(312) 644-1920

Books and Tapes Available

These self-help books and skill-building audiocassettes—on intimacy, self esteem, career advancement, achieving success-oriented goals, and creativity in the organizational setting—are valuable tools for individual self-improvement or for use by helping professionals in their work with clients. They also are useful classroom texts and seminar materials.

Both Dr. Dauw and therapist Regina Balutis are available to speak to organizations, conventions, meetings, and seminars on problems of intimacy; how communication problems hinder people from leading healthy, rewarding lives; and practical steps one can take to develop a strong, affirming sense of self-esteem—the first building block on the road to communication, commitment, and supportive relationships.

Specific programs currently available for presentation are: Increasing Self-Esteem; Human Relations; Stress Reduction; Human Sexuality; and Personal Change Programs. For information on these and other programs, contact either Dr. Dauw or Ms. Balutis at 312-644-1920.

1. **THE STRANGER IN YOUR BED: A GUIDE TO EMOTIONAL INTIMACY** (Nelson-Hall, 1979), Dean Dauw, Ph.D. A practical, self-help book which explains—in everyday terms—how physical intimacy as an expression of love and caring is the first step on the road to emotional intimacy, and how a healthy sex life can become a source of personal comfort, happiness, and contentment. (hard cover)

$11.95 per copy

2. **SEX THERAPY INNOVATIONS** (Waveland 1984), Dean Dauw, Ph.D. The surrogate technique is as highly controversial as it is successful. This book attempts to dissolve many of the misconceptions about this form of therapy which could help men and women learn to communicate sexually — intimately and openly. (paperback)

$5.00 per copy

3. INTIMACY: THE KEY TO BUILDING A SPECIAL RELATIONSHIP
(HRD, 1981), Dean Dauw, Ph.D., Dianna Bolen, M.A., and Michael
E. Carbine, M.A. A 6-tape, 6-hour audiocassette skill-building program
which discusses intimacy and its role in special relationships. Topics
include physical and emotional intimacy; autonomy within a partnership; communications; partnership roles; and self-esteem.

$45 per set

4. SELF-ESTEEM AND RISK TAKING FOR SUCCESS (HRD, 1982),
Dean Dauw, Ph.D. and Michael E. Carbine, M.A. A 2-tape, 2-hour
discussion of the ''success-type personality'' and the major traits and
characteristics that typically are found in successful people. The self-
help skill building series is designed to help you understand the
ingredients for success and to enhance your ability to achieve success-
oriented goals.

$10.95 per set

5. UP YOUR CAREER (3rd edition, Waveland, 1980), Dean Dauw, Ph.D.
A self-help book which discusses how to tap your inner resources and
improve your career potential, with several exercises and self-
evaluations for developing a goal achievement plan.

$9.95 per copy

6 CREATIVITY AND INNOVATION IN ORGANIZATIONS (4th
edition, Waveland Press, 1980) Dean Dauw, Ph.D. A practical discussion of recent research and theory about creativity and innovation in
executives, managers, and others working in the world of business.
The book also discusses organizational development and the process
that takes place when highly creative executives change careers.

$15.95 per copy

**(See Order Blank
on Reverse Side)**

Please send me the following:

_____ copies of book #1 (Stranger) @ $11.95: $ _____

_____ copies of book #2 (Sex Therapy) @ $5.00: $ _____

_____ sets of tape set #3 (Intimacy) @ $45.00: $ _____

_____ sets of tape set #4 (Success) @ $10.95: $ _____

_____ copies of book #5 (Career) @ $9.95: $ _____

_____ copies of book #6 (Creativity) @ $15.95: $ _____

_____ copies of **Feeling Better: Building Self Esteem** @ 6.95: $ _____

SubTotal: $ _____

Illinois Residents add 8% sales tax: $ _____

Total: $ _____

Ship to:

Name _____

Street Address _____

City_____ State _____ Zip _____

Payment enclosed ☐   **Charge my: VISA** ☐   **MasterCard** ☐

Card Number _____ Expiration Date _____

Signature _____

HRD, Inc.
Department S
112 West Oak Street
Chicago, IL 60610